Table of Contents

ROurke
Educational Media
rourkeeducationalmedia.com

A Division of
Carson
Dellosa
Education

Can you find these words?

chew

puppies

tail

wrinkles

Bulldog Puppies

puppies

These are Bulldog **puppies**!

What do Bulldog puppies look like?

They have a short **tail**.

tail

They have **wrinkles.**

6

They get bigger. They grow to 13 inches (33 centimeters) tall.

What do Bulldog puppies act like?

They like to **chew**.

They like people.

This puppy loves its family!

13

Did you find these words?

They like to **chew**.

These are Bulldog **puppies**!

They have a short **tail**.

They have **wrinkles**.

Photo Glossary

 **chew** (choo): To grind food between the teeth.

 **puppies** (PUHP-eez): Dogs that are young and not fully grown.

 **tail** (tayl): Part of an animal that sticks out at the back end.

 **wrinkles** (RING-kuhlz): Folds in the skin.

Index

About the Author

Hailey Scragg is a writer from Ohio. She loves all puppies, especially her puppy, Abe! She likes taking him on long walks in the park.

www.rourkeeducationalmedia.com

PHOTO CREDITS: cover: ©Liliya Kulianionak, ©manley099 (bone); back cover: ©onetouchspark (inset), ©Naddiya (pattern); pages 2, 3, 14, 15: ©Aly Tyler; pages 2, 4-5, 14, 15: ©jonathandowney; pages 2, 6-7, 14, 15: ©mrbig-photography; pages 8-9: ©badmanproduction; pages 2,10-11, 14, 15: ©Tera Images; pages 12-13: ©Vadim Zakharishchev

Edited by: Kim Thompson
Cover and interior design by: Janine Fisher

Library of Congress PCN Data
Bulldog Puppies / Hailey Scragg
(Top Puppies)
ISBN 978-1-73162-862-6 (hard cover)(alk. paper)
ISBN 978-1-73162-861-9 (soft cover)
ISBN 978-1-73162-863-3 (e-Book)
ISBN 978-1-73163-341-5 (ePub)
Library of Congress Control Number: 2019944974

Printed in the United States of America,
North Mankato, Minnesota

LIFE OF ROSSETTI.

LIFE

DANTE GABRIEL ROSSETTI

BY

JOSEPH KNIGHT

KENNIKAT PRESS
Port Washington, N. Y./London

LIFE OF DANTE GABRIEL ROSSETTI

First published in 1887
Reissued in 1972 by Kennikat Press
Library of Congress Catalog Card No: 73-160765
ISBN 0-8046-1586-1

Manufactured by Taylor Publishing Company   Dallas, Texas

CONTENTS.

CHAPTER III.

CHAPTER IV.

CHAPTER V.

CHAPTER VI.

CHAPTER VII.

CHAPTER VIII.

CHAPTER IX.

CHAPTER X.

CHAPTER XI.

CHAPTER XII.

NOTE.

———•••———

IN the following compilation Rossetti is studied principally as a writer. With his paintings I have no
very extensive acquaintance, nor have I the ability to
pronounce upon them a judgment. Full use has been
made of the very valuable labours of my predecessors,
Mr. William Sharp and Mr. Hall Caine. I am glad to
acknowledge my great indebtedness to Mr. Ford Madox
Brown and Mr. William Rossetti for the privilege of
access to the correspondence of Rossetti, and, in the
case of the latter, for constant and most friendly services.
Early associates of Rossetti who now occupy a foremost
place in art and letters have been obligingly communica-
tive and kind, placing at my disposal letters and recollections. If I do not mention the names of those to whom
my warmest acknowledgments are due, it is because I do
not wish to make the porch too ornate and distinguished
for the edifice.

JOSEPH KNIGHT.

LIFE OF ROSSETTI.

CHAPTER I.

A S the name indicates, the family of Dante Gabriel Rossetti is of Italian origin. On the paternal side the painter-poet belongs to Vasto d'Ammone, the ancient Histonium, a small, secluded, and picturesquely situated city of the Abruzzi, on the Adriatic coast of the then kingdom of Naples. The name Rossetti, though borne in Italy by several men who attained eminence in painting or music was not originally that of the family to which it owes its highest honours. The primary name of this was Della Guardia. In a language overflowing with diminutives, the name Rossetti, indicating an original tendency to red hair, a characteristic which ceased to distinguish the family, was bestowed upon certain of its members. In compliance with a custom more common in Italy than in England, but not unknown here, what was originally applied as a nick-name became accepted as a patronymic. The poet's grandfather, Domenico Rossetti, was connected with the iron trade in his native city. His son, Gabriele Rossetti, subsequently distinguished as a patriot and a man of letters, was born at Vasto, and proceeded to Naples, where he became a

custodian of ancient bronzes in what was then known
as the Bourbon Museum.   An eager advocate of the
liberties of his country, he was one of a body of
reformers by whom, in 1820, a Constitution was wrested
from Ferdinand, King of the Two Sicilies.   The return
of the monarch at the head of an Austrian army from
Laybach, whither he had been summoned to meet in
congress the Emperor of Austria, brought with it, to
the leaders in the movement, a " reign of terror."
Gabriele Rossetti, whose patriotic songs no less than
his actions, had made him an object of special ani-
mosity to the authorities, was, after a period of concealment, smuggled, in an English uniform, out of Naples
by the aid of the admiral of the English fleet in the
Bay.   In 1822 he arrived safely in Malta, where he
remained until 1825, when, furnished with introductions
by the governor, John Hookham Frere, whose friendship
he had secured, he proceeded to London.   In the year
after his arrival he married Frances Mary Lavinia
Polidori, a lady of mixed Italian and English birth,
being the daughter by an English mother, whose maiden
name was Pierce, of Gaetano Polidori, the translator of
Milton, somewhile secretary of Alfieri, the dramatist,
and sister of Dr. Polidori, who in 1816, as a physician,
accompanied Byron to Geneva.   Appointed in 1831 to
the post of Professor of Italian Literature at King's
College, Gabriele Rossetti relinquished that post in
1845 in consequence of failure of sight.   He lived nine
years longer, dying on April 26, 1854.   He wrote
many works in prose and verse, the best known in
England being his "Comento Analitico sulla Divina

Comedia," 1826-27 : "Sullo Spirito Anti-Papale," 1832 ;
and "Il mistero dell' amor platonico," 1840. In those of
his works dealing with Dante he strenuously advocated
the view that the character of Beatrice is allegorical, and
is designed to serve as a vehicle for political, theological,
and social theories. In Dante and other poets of his
cycle he divined an intention, under the veil of poetical
and allegorical expression, to attack the Papacy. These
views, it is needless to say, have not passed unchallenged.
In Italy, and especially in his own district, the name of
Gabriele Rossetti is held in high reverence and affection
for his services to the cause of liberty. A medal has
been struck in his honour. Centenary commemorations
were held in 1883. His house was purchased as public
property. The noble market-place in his native town,
formerly known as the Piazza del Pesce, is named after
him, the Piazza Gabriele Rossetti, and is intended to
contain a statue to his memory ; and the theatre is called
in his honour Teatro Comunale Rossetti. Mrs. Rossetti
meanwhile survived her son, dying April 8, 1886.

Four children were born to Gabriele and Frances
Rossetti. These are all honourably known in connection with literature. Maria Francesca, the author of
" A Shadow of Dante," was the eldest. Dante Gabriel,
who was born on the 12th of May, 1828, at 38, Charlotte Street, Great Portland Place, London, came next in
order. He was originally called after his father, his godfather, Charles Lyell, father of the eminent geologist,
and the great Italian poet,—Gabriel Charles Dante.
William Michael, the poet and critic ; and Christina, the
inspired author of " Goblin Market," " The Prince's

Progress," and other works in prose and verse, complete the list, having been born respectively in 1829 and 1830.

Concerning the early life of Rossetti little is preserved. After receiving some instruction at a private school in Foley Street, Portland Place, where, he stayed from the autumn of 1836 to the summer of 1837, he went to King's College School, where he remained until 1843, receiving an education in Latin, French, and the rudiments of Greek. In Italian he was naturally proficient, and such portions of his correspondence with his father as survive are in that language. A certain knowledge of German he acquired at home. His taste for literature was developed at an early age. When five years old he wrote a so-called drama which he entitled "The Slave," the two characters in which were respectively entitled Slave and Traitor. In or about his thirteenth year he began a romantic prose tale called "Roderick and Rosalba." Towards the close of his schooldays, "Sir Hugh the Heron : a Legendary Tale," in four parts, by Gabriel Rossetti, junr., founded upon a tale by Allan Cunningham, was privately printed by his maternal grandfather, Gaetano Polidori. Little in this work, a copy of which is in the British Museum, shows signs of more than common promise. It is not included in his collected works, and has hitherto escaped the attention of the grubbers after early productions of genius. That it will finally avoid being unearthed and reprinted is scarcely to be hoped. Apprehensive of the result, Rossetti—who had strong views on the subject, and held that the portion of a writer's work which he himself intended for publication should alone be given to the world—placed on record, in a common-place book, the history of the growth of the poem, and the record of his opinion that it was destitute of ordinary juvenile promise. Before quitting school the desire to be a painter had taken possession of him. After the summer vacation of 1843, accordingly, Rossetti, instead of returning to school, began his technical education in art at Cary's art academy, in Bloomsbury. The earliest of his letters which has been preserved is dated September 1, 1842, from Chalfont, St. Giles, where he was staying with his uncle, a solicitor, who had anglicized his name to Henry Polydore. It is addressed to his mother, with whom he maintained the most affectionate relations, and marks the commencement of a correspondence with the same dearly-prized relative, in which all that is brightest and best in his nature comes out. A positive adoration for his mother animated Rossetti through his life. To the closing days he owned her influence upon his literary opinions and verdicts; her beliefs were to him matters of reverence. To please or to amuse her he employed all the resources of his intellect; describing for her scenes and characters, treasuring up records of the behaviour of animals, depicting with poetic vividness the features around him, and rarely failing, when he was in the country, to deluge her with flowers. From the first communication we get some insight into the boy's character and his intellectual growth. After dismissing the house associated with Milton as unquestionably the ugliest and dirtiest in the village, he describes his reading or his attempts to read. First he begins "The Infidel's Doom," by Dr. Bird, but is unable to finish the perusal. No more success attends an attempt to read Walpole's "Castle of Otranto," and the young student at the period of writing is deep in Defoe's "History of the Plague." He announces his intention, for the benefit of his sister Maria, to make a sketch of the church which he thinks pretty, and then indulges in some banter on his mother's assumed uneasiness because he has started without a Prayer Book, and assures her that his uncle's "swearing book"—that is, the book on which oaths were taken—will answer all purposes. It may be here noted that the Rossettis, though descended from Italian and Catholic families, were brought up as Protestants. Gabriele Rossetti's feud with the Papacy made him tolerant of any dissent from Catholicism. Miss Polidori meanwhile was the daughter of an English mother, and by an arrangement—more common in those days than it has since become—the sons were brought up in the father's religion, and the daughters in that of the mother. Mrs. Rossetti remained to her death a devout Protestant, and her son manifested a constant respect for her views. At this early age the taste of the collector, by which Rossetti was always strongly influenced, asserted itself. In conjunction with his brother he commenced to illustrate with purchased engravings the Waverley Novels, and he complains that his Christmas boxes have all been spent in the acquisition of prints. He also collected illustrations to Shakespeare and Byron. The following year he is at 50, Charlotte Street, to which house, from 38 in the same street, his family have removed. He is following assiduously his profession, and tells how he has just finished studying the bones, and that his next drawing will probably be an anatomy figure. He is much struck by the exhibition at Westminster of the cartoons for the Houses of Parliament, which he pronounces, with juvenile enthusiasm, "a splendid sight," preferring it to the exhibition of the Royal Academy. Among the cartoons which win his special praise are Armitage's Landing of Julius Cæsar in Britain ; Watts' Caractacus led Captive, which is his first favourite ; and Boadicea addressing her Army, by Selous ; Severn's Queen Eleanor sucking the Poison from her Husband's Arm, he pronounces "almost completely wanting in expression ; " and he condemns a Signing of the Magna Charta as " the work of a child." In the fact that the works exhibited are by young painters, he finds a vindication of English art, and he opposes the accusation that artists of the English school clothe their figures overmuch, in order, by attracting attention to outside ornament—satin, jewels, and cloth of gold in the highest state of finish—to hide their ignorance of anatomy. These opinions of a lad of fifteen are crude in some respects ; they are, however, wanting neither in candour nor in insight.

At meetings of the Sketching Club, which he joins, he begins two sketches. These are The Death of Marmion, and The Old Soldier relating his Battles to the Parson from "The Deserted Village;" and he plans a third to be done, as he writes to his mother, who is in Paris, "in prime style," which shall represent the parting of two lovers. He also tells the same correspondent that he does not care, as yet, to go up to the Academy with a probation drawing and risk rejection.

Side by side with his art studies he continues his

literary efforts.   He is, he states, writing a romance
entitled " Sorrentino," of which all traces are lost.   The
tribulations of this ill-starred production are so many, and
so great, that, " if the approbation of others were the only
encouragement to an author to continue his literary
labours, the romance in question would long since have
found its way behind the grate."   His sister Maria
refuses, he complains, to listen to it.   On its completion,
however, he will offer it to some publisher, for, " defying
all accusation of vanity and self-esteem," he cannot help
considering that " it is equal to very many of the sense-
less productions which daily issue from the press "—a
modest meed of praise to which it might well be entitled.
At the close of the following year, and the beginning of
1845, he is at Boulogne, where he has an attack of small-
pox, from which fortunately he escapes unscarred.   His
enthusiasm is now in behalf of Gavarni, Tony Johannot,
and Nanteuil, whose works he assiduously collects.   His
study of literature is confined to the writings of French
novelists of the day, some of which he condemns for
their stupidity and obscenity.   The " Colomba " of
Prosper Mérimée excites, however, his extreme admiration.   It contains, he declares, some Corsican ballads
exactly in the style of the old English poetry.   One of
these, unfortunately a fragment, he so much admires, that
he has taken the trouble of translating it.   A supernatural
story called " La Vénus d'Ille " is " unutterably fine."   In
these verdicts the future author of " Rose Mary," " The
King's Tragedy," and " Sister Helen " may be foreseen.

   From this time until the beginning of the period of
his literary and artistic activity, his correspondence with

his mother and his brother languished, for no reason probably except that he was at home and had no need to write. In 1846 he was admitted to the Antique School of the Royal Academy. The life school of the same institution he never attended. He appears to have worked hard, if spasmodically. His attendance at the school of art must have been fairly regular. He tells us how, after consuming a frugal meal at some street stall, he has been at a class by six o'clock. Concurrently with his art occupations, moreover, he " kept his hand in " at poetry by writing original verses and translations from the Italian and the German. Indications of his future development are afforded in the selection of German works for translation. These included passages from the " Niebelungen Lied," which remained a favourite subject of conversation with him even when his knowledge of German had faded, and the whole of the tender and gracious " Arme Heinrich," of Hartmann von Auë, the Swabian Crusader and Minnesinger, now included under the title " Henry the Leper," in the second volume of his collected works. Of his life at this and a previous time he spoke in subsequent days with little enthusiasm. To his friend and biographer, Mr. Hall Caine, he described himself as deficient in youth and physical courage, and disinclined to take part in school games or in boyish quarrels, " not without generous impulse, but in the main selfish of nature, and reclusive in habit of life." So far as regards the latter portion of this statement, it was in part assumably true. The whole can only be accepted as the estimate of a man of introspective habits, who mistakes

for timidity a keen sense of danger. Through his entire
life Rossetti, though fond of walking, showed little disposition to violent exertion. He was, however, sustained
and resolute when action was forced upon him, and on
one or two occasions when unexpected peril presented
itself he showed himself brave and collected. These
qualities do not come at call. Reclusive in life, and in
some respects inert in his youth, he probably was ; but
cowardice, and selfishness in its larger acceptance, could
never have been numbered among his defects.

CHAPTER II.

A T his father's house Rossetti had met poets, scholars, and patriots, and had acquired that knowledge of Italian literature, and especially of Dante and his cycle, which was to bear ripe fruit in his following life. At the Academy he came under the personal influence of men such as Mr. Holman Hunt, Sir John Millais, and Mr. Thomas Woolner. He seems for a while to have hesitated between literature and art. Mr. Holman Hunt, in his interesting papers on the Pre-Raphaelite Brotherhood, states that Rossetti had sent specimens of his poems to Leigh Hunt, with a request that he would read them and counsel the author as to the expediency of turning to literature as a profession. While speaking in complimentary terms of the poems, Leigh Hunt in his reply had strongly dissuaded the young aspirant from adopting the profession of poetry as "too pitiable to be chosen in cool blood." At this time, moreover, the influence of Rossetti over those around him, the extent and power of which constitutes one of the most remarkable aspects of his individuality, and can neither be measured nor very easily credited by those to whom he was wholly unknown, had asserted itself. He had, even then, at the Academy, "a following" of those whom Mr. Holman

Hunt, not too sympathetically, describes as "noisy students."

In March, 1848, Rossetti, who had been greatly struck with the work of Mr. Ford Madox Brown, wrote to him requesting permission to attend his studio as pupil. In the letter making the request he warmly praises Mr. Madox Brown's paintings, especially his Parisina and Giaour, and says that if he ever does anything on his own account, it will be under the influence of such inspiration. This application of an enthusiastic youth to one but seven years his senior met with courteous acceptance. Rossetti accordingly commenced to paint in Mr. Madox Brown's studio, not as a paying pupil, but as a friend, and laid, in so doing, the foundation of a close friendship, amounting almost to brotherhood, which extended over, and greatly influenced, his subsequent life. His intimacy with Mr. William Bell Scott, like himself, poet and painter, began even earlier, and was scarcely less active for good. It was, however, as a poet, not as a painter, that Mr. Scott was approached. By various poems contributed by Mr. Scott to magazines Rossetti had been profoundly struck. With that feeling of brotherhood to all aiming high in literature or art, which to the end remained a striking characteristic, Rossetti wrote to the author of these compositions, expressing his admiration for them, and enclosing some of his own poems. The letter thus sent is dated 25th November, 1847, and signed Gabriel Charles Rossetti. Mr. Scott, who was at that time in Newcastle, was greatly struck with the verses, and, after his return to London, a friendship, which proved close and enduring, was formed.

While working in the studio of Mr. Madox Brown, Rossetti executed his first oil painting—a portrait of his father. This was in 1847. In the same year he took, jointly with Mr. Holman Hunt, a studio in Cleveland Street, close to Howland Street, Fitzroy Square. Among the traces of this association admirers of Mr. Holman Hunt will find, in that artist's famous picture of Rienzi swearing revenge over the body of his brother, the portrait of Rossetti, who sat for Rienzi. It may be mentioned, also, that in Sir John Millais' well-known picture of the same epoch, Lorenzo and Isabella, Mr. William Rossetti sat for the principal figure, and Dante Gabriel Rossetti for a guest who is seen drinking. The meeting of these fervid youths, devoted to the study and practice of painting and poetry, led naturally to schemes for the regeneration of the art they loved, and to the foundation of a species of *cénacle*, as, after the cœnaculum, or chamber in which was held the Last Supper, Sainte-Beuve, E. and A. Deschamps, Gautier, and other founders of what is known in France as Romanticism, elected to call themselves in sign of their worship of Victor Hugo. This later *cénacle* was destined to exercise an influence far more durable than such institutions, constantly sneered at and disparaged, but always interesting, often exhibit. The date when the Pre-Raphaelite Brotherhood was established was the autumn of 1848. This was not the only scheme which the young blood, "brisk as the April birds in primrose season," had excogitated. One mad idea which Rossetti ventilates at this period deserves to be mentioned as anticipating in a remarkable manner a portion of Mr. Robert Louis Stevenson's brilliant romance, the " New Arabian Nights." It is propounded by Rossetti to his brother and close ally, writing to whom he says : " *Apropos* of death, Hunt and I are going to get up among our acquaintances a mutual suicide association, by the regulations of which every member being weary of life may call at any time upon another to cut his throat for him. It is all, of course, to be done very quietly, without weeping or gnashing of teeth. I, for instance, am to go in and say, ' I say, Hunt, just stop painting that head for a minute and cut my throat,' to which he will respond by telling the model to keep the position, as he shall only be a moment, and, having done his duty, will proceed with the painting." If there is any one to whom this wild pleasantry seems distasteful, it must be remembered that its originators were lads of twenty, or thereabouts, whose schemes shortly afterwards all but revolutionised art, and who, before they reached the age at which the responsibilities of manhood are supposed to begin, were to see themselves pilloried for work which their enemies could neither equal nor grasp. In the spring of 1849 Rossetti had painted The Girlhood of Mary Virgin, Mr. Holman Hunt the great picture of Rienzi, and Sir John Millais the Lorenzo and Isabella, which Mr. Holman Hunt justly calls " the most wonderful painting that any youth still under twenty years of age ever did in the world." Mr. Holman Hunt attributes the shape taken by the ideas of revolt, then surging in his own mind and in that of Rossetti, to the sight at the house of Millais of a book of engravings of the frescoes in the Campo Santo at Pisa. " The Life and Letters of Keats " of Lord Houghton, to the perusal of which by himself and Rossetti, during a visit together to Rochester and Blackheath, Mr. Hunt refers, must also be credited with an influence in the same direction. According to Mr. Hunt, this appears to have been earlier in date than the inspection at Millais' of the book of frescoes.

On the 20th of August, 1848, Rossetti speaks of himself and Hunt as settled down (in the studio) "quite comfortably," and says that his companion is engaged upon the preparations for his Rienzi. He refers to his not having yet got through the first volume of " The Life of Keats," and continues, " He seems to have been a glorious fellow —and says in one place (to my great delight) that having just looked over a folio of the first and second schools of Italian painting, he has come to the conclusion that some of the early men surpassed even Raphael himself."

In the same letter he states that he went with Hunt to Woolner's " the other evening," where, on what he calls the alternate principle, they composed a poem of twenty-four stanzas. Facility in verse writing had long been a gift of Rossetti. In their home at Charlotte Street, he, William, and their sister Christina had been accustomed to *bouts rimés*, or verses written to rhymes previously supplied, and other forms of composition. At this time, however, Rossetti, who had already written many of his most remarkable compositions, including several of the translations from Dante and poets of his cycle, " My Sister's Sleep " and " The Blessed Damozel," stood fully equipped in poetic accomplishment. It would, however, be a matter of extreme interest if the poem composed by three such men, supposing it not to have been mere banter, as perhaps it was, could be traced. Rossetti unfortunately neglects to give the name.

That the present century has witnessed in art and letters a second renaissance, or period of new birth, neither less remarkable nor less potent than that heralded or marshalled by the discovery of printing, has recently been borne in upon men's minds. In this renewal of life the Pre-Raphaelite movement is at once a manifestation and an influence. It has been pointed out by different writers, and nowhere more clearly and forcibly than by Mr. Theodore Watts, in the brilliant essay upon Rossetti he contributes to the "Encyclopædia Britannica," that the secret of what the writer calls the Renascence of Wonder consists in going back from the "temper of imitation, prosaic acceptance, pseudo-classicism and domestic materialism" to the "temper of wonder, reverence, and awe." Within certain limitations this is true, as it is finely said. Between the period of Milton, in whom the "temper" last spoken of was only disturbed by political and theological obsession, and Blake, in whom it manifested its reviving influence, there interposed practically a century and a half, during which poetry was narrowed to the careful observance of traditions, to a sacrifice of essence to form, and to an apparently cynical contempt for whatever in the world breathes the spirit of romance and mystery. Though this space, compared with the long Polar night of ignorance which followed the conquest of civilization by barbarism, seems but short, it is probably enough to justify the view that regards it as death. It is possible, however, that in a subsequent age, those who from a more remote stand-point have a wider view may see in this period but the ebb of a great wave. It may, at least, be maintained that the malign influence over our literature in post-Shakespearean times has been French. To trace the causes by which the spirit of the first Renaissance, nowhere more active than among the southern French, was quenched by the joint persecutions of the Parliament and the Sorbonne, until the great upheaval of the sixteenth century was absolutely arrested, and from Ligugé, the seat of Geoffroi d'Estissac, the enlightened bishop of Maillezais, and patron of Rabelais, and the early French reformers, the brilliant company of dreamers and workers, who were the last hope of France, went forth to die on the Place de Grêves, to seek shelter at Geneva, or to perish of want or suicide in alien lands, is a subject for a volume rather than a paragraph. Up to the stake—"*Jusq'au feu exclusivement*"—Rabelais, joking upon the restrictions upon his practice of surgery imposed upon him as an ecclesiastic, who was not allowed to cut or to cauterize, said he would carry his revelation of truth. So far as this exactly went freedom of thought in France, and it needed the tocsin of St. Bartholomew, and the axe of Richelieu, to leave French life and literature what they became in the late seventeenth, and in the eighteenth centuries.

English literature, meanwhile, which after the flood time of the Elizabethan and Jacobean drama had ebbed into affectations and conceits, took under the Restoration its colour from France. Beneath a king a pensioner on the French monarch, it was not surprising to see Courtier-Poets under the like obligation to French

wits. With the cessation of French influence the national
spirit reasserted itself, and such external sway as has
been felt during the present century has been largely due
to Teutonic and Scandinavian literature, with which our
own, at its best, has constantly been associated. To his
familiarity with the Italian poets Rossetti added, as
has been seen, some knowledge of German literature. He was, moreover, well read in the old ballads
and romances. The last-named productions he used to
read, apart from the pleasure he took in their perusal, for
the purpose of enriching his vocabulary. It is only in
recent years that great writers have been seen, as in the
case of Victor Hugo and of Rossetti, deliberately to seek
in such fashion to enrich their style. The French poet,
it is known, rarely dealt in his fictions with any form of
labour or occupation without acquiring an acquaintance
with its innermost and most technical vocabulary, the
result being at times a little perplexing to the English
student who wishes to follow every word of Victor Hugo,
and does not always find a dictionary that will assist him.
Unconscious, meanwhile, of the existence of this precedent, Rossetti was employed at the British Museum
reading romances of chivalry, in the hope to "pitch
upon stunning words for poetry." To his brother he
states that he has "found several," and has also received
much enjoyment from the romances themselves, some of
which he declares to be "tremendously fine."

Rossetti, accordingly, apart from his gifts of imagination
and expression, was well stocked with the kind of literature most likely to fructify under existing conditions. He
was familiar also with the English poets of the previous

half-century, was an enthusiastic admirer of Byron, and had come under the influence of Mr. Browning, from whose works, which he had purchased, he was accustomed to quote. To these things must be added the before-mentioned power of inspiring enthusiasm and making proselytes, a power which, according to Mr. Holman Hunt, he appears to have exercised to an inconvenient extent, and to which, in his own despite, Mr. Hunt himself was compelled to yield ; an unfailing memory for any poetry that won his admiration, and (Mr. Hunt again) " a voice rarely equalled for simple recitations." Yet one more possession, rarest, perhaps, of all, has to be chronicled. This was an ungrudging, outspoken, loyal, and unselfish delight in the work of others, combined with a capacity and a disposition to bestow that praise, at once thoroughly appreciative and yet distinguishing, which to the artist temperament brings the keenest of pleasures.

Thus equipped, Rossetti, it may fairly be supposed, was, from the poetical side at least, the dominant influence in the establishment of the Pre-Raphaelite Brotherhood. That a picture of Mr. Holman Hunt, The Eve of Saint Agnes, formed the *point de départ*, or start-point, Mr. Hunt has told us, and is known from other sources. That Mr. Hunt also was the first to realize the purity of work in the early Italian painters, and that before he knew either of his subsequent associates, he had set to work to rival the sincerity of handling of the artists he admired, is also conceded. As stated by Mr. Ruskin, in after times their eloquent and sustained advocate, the aim of the Pre-Raphaelites was to " paint nature as it is around them, with the help of modern science." It is doubtful whether the leaders of the movement, glad as they were of the advocacy of their brilliant ally, were altogether content with the description of their aim. Without venturing on the dangerous ground of a definition, this aim may be said to have been to divest art of conventionality, to work with sincere purpose, and to reproduce with scrupulous fidelity all objects in animate and inanimate nature.

So far as regards Rossetti, it is easy to over-estimate the influence of Pre-Raphaelitism upon his work. At the outset, however, the idea commended itself warmly to him. He was at this period full of schemes of work and of worship. One scheme, suggestive of Comte, but probably owing nothing to him, to which he appears to have won the assent of his companion, Mr. Hunt, was the establishment of a "Set of Immortals." The full hierarchy has never been given to the world. The first rank was, however, reserved for Shakespeare and Jesus Christ.

CHAPTER III.

IN the studio jointly occupied by Mr. Hunt and Rossetti, the two artists began the pictures in which their new faith was to be shown to the world through their works. Mr. Hunt's picture, as is known, was the Rienzi swearing Revenge over the Body of his Brother. Rossetti's was The Girlhood of Mary Virgin. Working with them, in his own studio, was Sir John Millais, whose adhesion to their new creed the young associates had obtained. His contribution consisted of his picture from Keats' " Lorenzo and Isabella."

With the exhibition, in 1849, of these three pictures, a ferment in artistic and literary circles, destined to outlast the cause to which it owed its birth, took place. The signification of the three letters, P.R.B., or Pre-Raphaelite Brother, indicative of aims such as have previously been mentioned, which the painters affixed to their names, had been revealed by Rossetti to friends, one of whom gave it to the world. A storm of indignation was aroused among those against whose practice in art the new school was a protest. Writers were, of course, found to declaim with customary zeal against innovation, and as has generally been the case, especially in England, under similar conditions, the leaders of the new heresy were regarded as offenders against most things that are sacred or of good repute.

It is possible now to smile at the pother that was raised. The movement, which had in fact been anticipated by Mr. Madox Brown, was originated by young men, of whom the oldest was barely of age. Its influence, as a protest, was enduring, its tendency was beneficial, and the men, nurtured in its faith, however much they may have diverged from their first convictions, have attained the foremost places in their art. Whatever was extravagant or fantastic in view, might, and should, have been treated at the worst with banter. Time has vindicated the aim and the exertions of the Pre-Raphaelites, and nothing but shadows are now left for their antagonists to fight. At the outset, moreover, much useful support from outside sources was enlisted on their behalf. The active advocacy of Mr. Ruskin was of course invaluable to them. Other champions espoused their cause, and from the ranks of painters of established fame came some who perceived what was noble in their aim and stedfast in their work. Out of the Royal Academy, even, sprang encouragement and aid, by which one at least of the sorely pressed evangelists of a new doctrine was enabled to keep the wolf from the door, and proceed with his mission.

Before dealing with the short-lived magazine, which was put forward less as an "Apologia" than as a "Manifestation of Faith," it seems worth while to point to the outcome of Pre-Raphaelitism, so far as regards its principal exponents.

This is debateable ground, and the decisions here given are open to be challenged. Dealing only with works of primary importance, it will be found that Rossetti painted in oil, in accordance with his Pre-Raphaelite principles, The Girlhood of Mary Virgin, An Annunciation, otherwise known as Ecce Ancilla Domini, and the woman's face and the white calf in Found, a noble work, which, unfortunately, remains unfinished. From this time (1853) his work in this medium, while preserving its poetic and imaginative style of design and colouring, had no claim to be considered Pre-Raphaelite. It can indeed, with its strongly marked individuality, be forced into no class.

Sir John Millais continued faithful until 1855, and, so to speak, coquetted with his former love until 1856–57, after which he reverted to free handling and broader treatment. Among his latest works in the Pre-Raphaelite style are the Portrait of Ruskin, The Blind Girl, The Wounded Child on a Tomb, and The Vale of Rest. Some traces of Pre-Raphaelitism are also found in The Return of the Dove to the Ark. Mr. Holman Hunt may, then, claim to be the Abdiel of Pre-Raphaelitism, to which, while informing it with an assertive and priceless individuality, his art still belongs.

Other painters belonged, however, to the school so soon as it was formed, and by a curious irony of Fate, some who are now held the most representative among Pre-Raphaelites, were never, nominally at least, in its ranks.

Among the first Pre-Raphaelite painters was Mr. F. G. Stephens, now eminent as an art critic, at the time an eloquent defender of the views of the Brotherhood, towards the members of which, even to the present day, he has shown an exemplary loyalty. He was at that time an intimate friend of Mr. Holman Hunt, and warmly espoused the cause. His early paintings were Pre-Raphaelite, but his vocation for writing overpowering that for painting, he gave up the brush for the pen.

Walter Deverell was one of the most enthusiastic votaries whom the eloquence of Rossetti, and the example of Mr. Holman Hunt, seduced, and was, after a time, enrolled a probationary member. So exquisite a sense of simplicity and grace had this young painter, combined with a close fidelity to nature, that his premature death was a loss not only to Pre-Raphaelitism, but to art in general.

Charles Allston Collins painted for a time in the same manner, but was never a member of the Brotherhood. He failed to satisfy himself with his work, and after a time abandoned art for literature, in which he made a reputation.

James Collinson, the artist, was a Pre-Raphaelite Brother, and in addition to the artistic capacity, displayed in his youth great poetic capacity. He resigned his membership, however, after a short period, having joined the Catholic Church, with an idea, subsequently abandoned, of entering the priesthood.

Mr. Woolner, R.A., the sculptor, through his contributions to *The Germ*, was associated with the Brotherhood of which he was a member. His connection with it did not, however, extend far beyond his poems which appeared in that periodical, and his friendship with the artists, and his admiration for their works. His labours bear no traces of its influence. The connection of Mr. E. L. Bateman was the same, *minus* the contributions to *The Germ.*

Bernhard Smith, a sculptor, was closely bound up with the founders of the new faith. He went, in 1852, to Australia, where he died a couple of years ago.

Mr. Arthur Hughes was also an intimate of some of the Brotherhood.

Mr. William Bell Scott became a close, warm, and constant friend of Rossetti and other members of the Pre-Raphaelite Brotherhood. At the period when they first exhibited, he had been an exhibitor for nine years, and his imputed connection with the school is purely imaginary.

Thomas Seddon was carried away by the movement, but had no share in the initiative.

Two men, neither of them Pre-Raphaelites, remain to be mentioned. The first is Mr. Ford Madox Brown. An exhibitor since 1841, he did more to influence the Pre-Raphaelites than any other. Mr. Sharp, in his "Life of Rossetti," says, "If Dante Rossetti be considered the father of Pre-Raphaelitism, Mr. Madox Brown may be considered its grandfather." His sympathy with aspirations he helped to form was naturally keen, and the only cause of his not becoming a member of the Brotherhood was his disbelief in the advantage of cliques. In no other painter, however, have the principles of Pre-Raphaelitism found earlier or abler exposition. It may almost be held that his great picture of Work is the absolute masterpiece of Pre-Raphaelite method. It is painted with a thoroughness, completeness, and sincerity not to be surpassed in any painting belonging to, or inspired by, the school.

Mr. Burne Jones did not take up painting as a profession until, in subsequent years, at Oxford, he came under the sway of Rossetti, to whom indeed it is due that, abandoning the idea of entering the Church, he became a painter. The influence of Rossetti was strong upon him, and his method has much in common with that of the Pre-Raphaelites, as one of whom he is often, but mistakenly regarded. There were then in all seven Pre-Raphaelite Brethren—six artists, viz. : Holman Hunt, Rossetti, Millais, Woolner, James Collinson, and F. G. Stephens, and one literary member, the critic and poet, Mr. William Rossetti, who should yet be the laureate of the Brotherhood.

It is singular as well as gratifying to see how much virility as well as genius there was in the band. Collinson, the one weakling, vacated a seat which he was never qualified to fill. With that exception, the Brotherhood continued to do work of the highest class for thirty-four years, when Rossetti, at the close of a brilliant career, died, prematurely after all, his health ruined by indulgence in narcotics. What noble work in painting or sculpture is due to surviving members, Sir John Millais, Mr. Holman Hunt, and Mr. Woolner, and in poetry to the last-named, is known to the world at large. The knowledge of the fitness of some of their associates to rank with them is confined to a limited public. It is at least difficult to treat with ridicule or contempt a faith out of which such results have sprung, and it is a vindication of hard work, that five out of seven of the men who, thirty-seven or thirty-eight years ago, inaugurated a great movement, are still at the height of their productive powers, and in the foremost places in public estimation.

CHAPTER IV.

A NEW creed requires a new evangel. This it was an early aim of the Brotherhood to supply. The idea of a magazine, in which by letter-press and illustration, the views of the *cénacle* should be put forth, was Rossetti's. His own family, on the aid of which he might depend, supplied him with three poets. From the moment the scheme was formed, Rossetti, with characteristically sanguine faith, set to work for its realization. Material in abundance for a start was in existence. The forces, were, however, ill-drilled, the commissariat needed attention, and the ammunition even was adequate rather for a skirmish than a campaign. One evening in September, 1849, in a studio which Rossetti had taken in Newman Street, the arrangements with regard to the forthcoming publication were made, and the name of *The Germ*, suggested by Mr. William Cave Thomas, was adopted. William Rossetti, then aged barely twenty, was nominated to the editorship.

Some difficulty was experienced in inducing the editor to undertake the functions assigned him. The original intention was to announce the new publication as conducted by artists. This, of course, was prohibitive of the editorship being assigned to William Rossetti. This portion of the project was, however, abandoned, and the words " conducted by artists " were struck from the projected title-page.

Rossetti's correspondence with his brother at this period is full of the projected magazine.   On September 26th he starts with Mr. Holman Hunt on a long projected trip to Paris, and he sends his brother from Boulogne, on the 28th, a poem, "Upon the Cliffs—Noon," as well as some extracts from the book of Job, in writing out which he had found employment during a rough passage.   Previous to his departure, however, he had communicated much information of interest, stating that he hopes that he has found a publisher in Messrs. Aylott and Jones, of Paternoster Row, to whom he had been introduced by "a printer, a friend of Hancock's;" that the proprietors, by which he means the speculators, amount to about nine, including Hancock (a young sculptor of repute) and Herbert (Mr. J. R. Herbert, R.A.), who he fears, however, "is rather a doubtful case;" that Stephens is writing for the first number an article on early art, which he (Rossetti) has not seen, and that Hunt, who is now "tremendously agog about the thing," is "at his etching."   Somewhat doubtfully he suggests that "Old Collinson" should be induced to take a share, and urges his brother to impress this obligation upon such amount of mind as "Old Collinson" possesses.   Woolner, he also states, is going with him into the country.   This scheme was never carried into effect.   Mr. Woolner was, however, induced by his energetic young friend to contribute to the new periodical.   He was, indeed, warmly assured by Rossetti that his poem, " My Beautiful Lady," which appeared in the first number of *The Germ*, was written on the true Pre-Raphaelite lines.

His great piece of news is, however, that Mr. Coventry Patmore, to whom *it* (assumably the projected first number) was shown, seemed considerably impressed in its favour, and was even induced thereby to contribute to it a little poem of three stanzas, which, in order not to inflict upon his brother the agony of hope deferred, he copies out. The poem is that which, under the title of " The Seasons," appears on page 19 of the first number of *The Germ*.

This poem Rossetti, with pardonable warmth, pro-nounces, in a characteristic form of expression, "stun-ning." His jubilancy is, however, checked by the fact that Patmore, who does not intend to figure in any periodical until his new book of poems is out, withholds permission to publish his name.

These particulars, of no special importance in them-selves, are interesting as illustrations of the eagerness and impetuosity of Rossetti's nature, and of the power he possessed of winning over to his own views the generous minds with which he was thrown into contact. It may be mentioned as showing the state of mind in which, at this period of *The Germ*, its founder was, that his letters from Paris disclose views in art which, whatever their value, were much modified in his later years.

After complaining to his brother of Hunt spoiling his writing paper in attempts "to concoct an undecipherable monogram of P.R.B., to be signed to passports," &c., and sending a variety of sonnets, written on the top of

Notre Dame and elsewhere, he delivers his opinions on the paintings he has seen. At the Luxembourg "there are the following really wonderful pictures, viz. : two by Delaroche, two by Fleury, one by Ingres, and one by Hesse ; others by Scheffer, Granet, &c., are very good." The rest with a few exceptions the two travellers considered "trash." Delacroix, though, "almost worshipped" in Paris, incurs an eminently unfavourable verdict, except that his pictures " show a kind of savage genius."

In the Louvre there are a " most wonderful copy of a fresco by Angelico," a "tremendous " Van Eyck, " some mighty things by that real stunner, Leonardo," a "tremendous portrait by some Venetian," whose name he forgets, and a " stunning Francis I." by Titian. By Ingres he is puzzled. One picture in the Luxembourg is "unsurpassed for exquisite perfection " by anything he has seen. For others he would not give "two sous." "Now," he says, " for the best, Hunt and I solemnly decided that the most perfect work, taken *in toto*, that we have seen in our lives, are two pictures by Hippolyte Flandrin, representing Christ entering into Jerusalem, and His departure to death, hung in the Church of St. Germain des Près." After this expression he writes, " Wonderful ! wonderful ! wonderful ! "

On the 1st of January, 1850, the first number of *The Germ* was issued by Messrs. Aylott and Jones, of 8, Paternoster Row. Brilliant as are its contents, the poetical portion of them especially, the whole is, in a sense, juvenile. There is little in it to appeal to any but an esoteric circle. A sonnet, by Mr. William Rossetti, printed on the cover of the four numbers, conveyed in

lines richer in thought than music the principles to advocate which the magazine was started.   On the back of the
second page of the cover appeared a species of prose
advertisement, embodying the views of the founders,
and forming a sort of substitute for a preface.   After
stating that " an attempt will be made, both intrinsically
and by review, to claim for poetry that place to which its
present development in the literature of the country so
emphatically entitles it," this continues in what may be
regarded as the Shibboleth of Pre-Raphaelitism, to state
that " the endeavour held in view throughout the writings
on Art, will be *to encourage and enforce an entire adherence
to the simplicity of nature;* and also to direct attention,
as an auxiliary medium, to the comparatively few works
which Art has yet produced in this spirit.   It need
scarcely be added that the chief object of the etched
designs will be to illustrate this aim practically, as far as
the method of execution will permit ; in which purpose
they will be produced with the utmost care and completeness."

In the third number the title of the periodical changed
to "*Art and Poetry* : Being Thoughts towards Nature.
Conducted principally by Artists."   The name of Dickin-
son and Co., of New Bond Street, appears before that of
Aylott and Jones.   The wording of the advertisement is
altered, the explanation contained in the most pregnant
passage being to the following effect : " With a view to
obtain the thoughts of Artists upon Nature as evolved in
Art, in another language besides their *own proper* one, this
periodical has been established.   Thus, then, it is not
open to the conflicting opinion of all who handle the

brush and palette, nor is it restricted to actual practitioners; but is intended to enunciate the principles of those who, in the true spirit of Art, enforce a rigid adherence to the simplicity of Nature, either in Art or Poetry, and consequently regardless whether emanating from practical Artists, or from those who have studied nature in the Artists' school."

In these two passages, not otherwise perhaps claiming to be reprinted, the aim of the Pre-Raphaelites at the commencement of their mission is declared concisely with their own lips. It may be noted that in the second extract, an oversight in the first, which must have been galling to the concoctors of the magazine, is corrected. In the earlier—while Art appears with all the dignity of a capital letter—nature, whom it was a chief purpose to extol, is not similarly honoured. The italics in the second extract appear in the original—those in the first do not.

The first number opens with two subtle poems, by which though only a fragment of the more important and beautiful poem into which the two were subsequently woven, the reputation, as a poet, of Mr. Thomas Woolner, was first established, "My Beautiful Lady," and "Of my Lady in Death," with a species of double etching, or etching in two parts, by Mr. Holman Hunt, each half of which illustrates a passage in one or other of the poems. Then follow an unsigned sonnet of Mr. Ford Madox Brown; a not very brilliant paper by Mr. J. L. Tupper, on "The Subject in Art"; Mr. Coventry Patmore's poem, "The Seasons," the right to publish which had gladdened the heart of Rossetti; and "Dream Lands," a delightful poem of Miss Christina Rossetti. Rossetti himself comes next with "My Sister's Sleep," a poem written towards 1847, and his prose allegory, "Hand and Soul." A readable and penetrative criticism of "The Bothie of Toper-na-Fuosich," of Arthur Hugh Clough, by Mr. William Rossetti, occupies with long quotations a space perhaps disproportionate. A characteristic sonnet, also by the editor, a poem by Mr. J. L. Tupper, decidedly Pre-Raphaelite in intention, and a short poem by Miss Christina Rossetti, complete a number of exceptional interest to students of literature and art, and unlike any literary venture ever attempted, but bearing signs of weakness, that those accustomed to estimate the chances of prolonged life, cannot fail to note. Without being still-born, the infant was at least barely *viable*, had scarcely the conformation and development essential to the pro-longing of life.

Upon the character and contents of the remaining three numbers it is needless to dwell. In *The Germ* Rossetti published twelve contributions, including the before-mentioned prose allegory, "Hand and Soul." Five of these are lyrics, "My Sister's Sleep;" "The Blessed Damozel," "From the Cliffs—Noon;" written as is before mentioned at Boulogne, and subsequently called "Sea Limits;" "The Carillon," inspired by the bells at Bruges, whither, in course of the journey with Mr. Holman Hunt, he had gone; and "Pax Vobis," afterwards entitled "World's Worth:" and six are sonnets, respectively called "A Virgin and Child," by Hans Memmling; "A Marriage of St. Katherine," by Hans Memmling; "A Dance of Nymphs," by Mantegna; "A Venetian

Pastoral," by Giorgione ; and two sonnets on "Angelica rescued from the Sea," by Ingres.

With the exception of "My Sister's Sleep," "The Blessed Damozel," and "Pax Vobis," these poems were the outcome of his recent journey. The two Memmlings, with which, naturally, he was deeply impressed, were seen at Bruges. The Angelica picture he studied in the Luxembourg, and the two remaining pictures in the Louvre.

Of the six sonnets four, with slight alterations, appear in the "Poems" (1870). The lyrics from *The Germ*, which are comprised in the same collection, are much altered and enlarged, the additions in one case doubling the length.

At this period, then, Rossetti's merits as a poet and a painter stood revealed. It was in the earlier respect he thought himself more plenarily endowed. The sense of shortcoming in form weighed upon him, and the conquest of difficulties in the employment of poetic phrase constituted to him more of a labour of love than his struggle to make up for neglect of drawing in his early years.

When in April, 1850, *The Germ* expired, it left Rossetti with a high reputation. The circle of his admirers was the narrowest, possibly, to which the knowledge of a man of equal eminence has often been confined. His friends and admirers were however the coming men. Most qualities of his future work were moreover adumbrated, if they were not revealed, in the poems already published. "The Blessed Damozel," which underwent subsequent alteration, remains unsurpassed in workmanship. "From the Cliffs " showed the insight into Nature's mysteries subsequently developed in most of his poems, and the sonnets evidenced already a mastery of workmanship such as few of his predecessors or contemporaries have surpassed.

It is easy to believe that the collapse of the short-lived periodical into which the young enthusiasts put their best, was a disaster as well as a mortification. The work was not all loss, however, and aided in establishing the position of many poets. Very much of the poetry that first saw the light in *The Germ* is now enshrined in works which the world, in Milton's phrase, " will not willingly let die ; " while it is an amusing though incomprehensible thing that the four parts on which contemporary criticism would scarcely waste a word, are now probably, from the bibliographical standpoint, among the costliest works of their epoch, the identical copy by aid of which the above-mentioned productions have been verified having cost many more pounds than the original work cost shillings.

Among the sonnets and poems reserved for the collected works, or still unpublished, which belong to the period 1848-50, some are on pictures seen in Paris. One sonnet is on the last of Paris, a second on the road from Brussels to Waterloo, and a third on the return journey. Of these, however, except the sonnet, "On the Road to Waterloo," Rossetti speaks in depreciatory terms. During his visit to Paris he was greatly impressed by the acting of Rachel, whom he saw in Adrienne Lecouvreur, the year of its first production at the Théâtre Français (1849). With characteristic enthusiasm, he declares himself "astounded" by her. His utterances concerning the stage are few. He speaks, however (3rd September, 1850), of having been the other night to see "The Legend of Florence" (of Leigh Hunt), and finding it much more poetical than he anticipated. Miss Glyn, by whom the part of Ginevra was played at Sadler's Wells, where Rossetti must have seen her, he declares to have been " Godlike.'

CHAPTER V.

OF the contributions to *The Germ*, one may be supposed to have something of an autobiographical
character. This is "Hand and Soul," in which an insight into the nature and aspiration of Rossetti may be
traced. The incidents and characters in this have often,
we are told, and sometimes to the amusement of the
author, been assumed to be true. Both are, in fact,
imaginary. No such painter as the hero, Chiaro dell'
Erma, ever lived; no such picture as the Figura Mistica
was ever painted. The number and position assigned the
work as 161 in the Sala Sessagona of the Pitti Palace, in
Florence, the Dr. Aemmster, to whose zeal and enthusiasm the writer in a note declares himself indebted for
the picture's place and designation, the pamphlet by the
same authority upon the tryptic, and two cruciform pictures at Dresden, the very conversation of the students
whose attention is drawn to the canvas by the writer's
continuous study of it, are things of the imagination.
Neither then, nor at any period of his life, had Rossetti
been in Italy. As a work of pure phantasy, "Hand and
Soul" has far more interest than it would possess as a
record, partial or complete, of observation and experience.

Into an early prose fiction an author not seldom puts more of his personality than is to be found in any subsequent work.

The hero of "Hand and Soul" is a painter, literally a Pre-Raphaelite. From early boyhood he endeavours "towards the imitation of any objects offered in nature." More even than his sinews, or the blood of his life, his "extreme longing after a visible embodiment of his thoughts" strengthens as his years increase, until he begins to "*feel faint in sunsets, and at the sight of stately persons.*" The italics are not in the original. Having heard of the famous Giunta Pisano, towards whom he experiences "much of admiration with, perhaps, a little of that envy which youth always feels until it has learned to measure success by time and opportunity," he offers himself as a pupil. He claims to be only a student, with nothing in the world "so much at his heart as to become that which he has heard told of him with whom he was speaking." He is "received with courtesy and consideration, and shown into the study of the famous artist. Once admitted within the sanctuary, he feels that the forms are lifeless and incomplete, and arrives, with a sudden sense of exultation, at the conclusion, "I am the master of this man." Defeated and disappointed, as it appears, rather than spurred to effort, he grows, after a while, torpid, and is seduced by the pleasures of a luxurious city, with "music in its groves," and with "great gardens laid out for pleasure," wherein "beautiful women" pass "to and fro."

Wonder seizes him that he has never "claimed his inheritance of those years in which his youth was cast."

He is well-favoured and very manly in his walking, with a glory upon his face "as upon the face of one who feels a light round his hair."

From his indulgence in pleasures, and his apathy with regard to art, he is roused by the reputation that is being acquired by a youth named Bonaventura, in whom Giunta Pisano has to fear a possible rival. He resumes work, accordingly, with diligence, "living entirely to himself." After nightfall he walks "abroad in the most solitary places, . . . hardly feeling the ground under him, because of the thoughts of the day," by which he is held in fever. The room contains, besides the matters of his art, a "very few books," a "small consecrated image of St. Mary Virgin, wrought out of silver," before which stands always in summer time "a glass containing a lily and a rose." He is, as a rule, calm and regular in study, but sometimes works through the whole of a day, "not resting once so long as the light lasted." At times, when he cannot paint, he sits "for hours in thought of all the greatness the world has known from of old, until he was weak with yearning, like one who gazes upon a path of stars."[1]

What follows is of no less interest as illustrating Rossetti's aims and theories of art, and for the key it affords to much subsequent workmanship. Read by the light of Rossetti's career, the revelation thus afforded is startling. He, however, is but a poor hand at piecing out imperfec-

---

[1] The extracts are taken from the story as it appears in *The Germ*, and not from the versions, different in some respects, which appeared in pamphlet form, in *The Fortnightly Review*, and in The Collected Works.

tions who cannot, from this sketch, draw a picture of the life
of the impetuous, yet dreamy student, to whose imaginative
temperament pleasure and work alike presented themselves in their most seductive aspects. While keenly
sensitive to the prick of that " spur which the clear spirit
doth raise," Rossetti was not one too early to despise or
to forget the delights which others " use "—

> " To sport with Amaryllis in the shade
>   Or with the tangles of Neæra's hair."

Much of what he ascribes to Chiaro dell' Erma is, of
course, his own experience. The aspirations which drove
his hero to be a painter are those by which he was himself stirred. The longing after a veritable embodiment of
his thoughts and the touch of growing faint, like Porphyro
in the chamber of Agnes, in sunsets, or at the sight of
stately persons, could come only as a revelation from
within. Like Chiaro dell' Erma, Rossetti sought for ad-
mission into the studio of the master whose work he
admired, and, like him, assumably, though without any
lessening of his admiration for his master, felt the dimi-
nution of enthusiasm that not seldom comes when the
desired in art as in other things becomes the possessed.
Like him, once more, it is fair to suppose he was stung
to further exertions by the success of some painter of his
own hour, his close associate, Mr. Holman Hunt, or
another, and began the career of work to which success
comes in most cases as a necessary response.

Supposing, even, that these coincidences are insignifi-
cant, such is not at least the picture of the aspects under
which pleasure presented itself, nor the association of

musical groves, and gardens laid out for delight, with the beautiful women, at whose sight the young pulse was stirred, and who, doubtless, were of the stately people at whose sight he grew faint.   These things, with the subsequent account of his nocturnal walks, then, doubtless infrequent, but afterwards familiar, supply a picture of his early life differing little, it may be, from that of many other youths of genius, but containing much not elsewhere to be found, and with many traits that are characteristic and individual.

In the literary work of this epoch there are some signs of youth and inexperience.   In "Hand and Soul," however, the language of which is sustainedly poetical, and in "The Blessed Damozel," which ranks with Rossetti's best accomplishments, the touch is firm and assured.   The opinions expressed concerning contemporary artists are not always those of his later years.   It is easy to understand how the purity and austerity of work, and the elevation of expression in the pictures of Hippolyte Flandrin which betray him into raptures should seem to him a justification of his own theories.   In subsequent days, however, Flandrin, with other objects of his juvenile adoration, was more judicially appraised.

CHAPTER VI.

ABOUT 1850, Rossetti, who had hitherto lived in his father's house in Charlotte Street, and worked in the studio of Mr. Madox Brown, in that in Cleveland Street which he shared with Mr. Holman Hunt, or in Newman Street, in a house part of which was occupied as a dancing saloon, or, as he jocularly called it, a "hop shop," took rooms at 14, Chatham Place, Blackfriars Bridge. In these rooms, now swept away, which were situated near the north-west corner of the bridge, and commanded a fine view of the Thames, an active and very productive portion of his life was spent, and it is with them that the romance of his life is associated. Though true to old friends and constant in former faith, new acquaintances were made, and the broadening influence of maturing years, independence, and friction with the world asserted itself. No long time after he was settled in his new quarters, he made the personal acquaintance of Browning, for whom he had a warm admiration, and to whom, when that poet was in Italy, he had written. Browning's poems, of which he was one of the earliest appreciators. furnished him with subjects, his first water-

colour painting, an illustration to Browning's " Laboratory," having been painted so early as 1849. Among
others, in addition to his Pre-Raphaelite friends, with
whom he was at this period intimate were James Hannay,
J. P. Seddon, Hancock, and Mr. Allingham.

To this change of life and widening of associations
may, perhaps, be assigned the blending with the mystical
and transcendental in his writings and paintings of the
romantic. The original sketch, now lost, of How They
Met Themselves, the design of which was not finished in
ink until 1860, while the water-colour painting belongs to
1864, was executed in 1851. To about the same period
belongs the ballad of " Sister Helen," which a year or two
later was printed, under the signature of H. H. H., in the
Düsseldorf Annual, by Mary Howitt, to whom, at her
request, he had sent it. That a striking change of
method and of view has come over the painter and the
poet between the production of The Girlhood of Mary
Virgin and " The Blessed Damozel," on the one hand, and
the inception of How They Met Themselves, and the
execution of " Sister Helen," will not be disputed. The
transition is not abrupt, and there are instances of recurrence to early manner and motives ; but it is effectual. It
is a subject of regret that the date of many of Rossetti's
poems is uncertain. During many years he entertained
the idea of publishing a volume of poems to be called
" Dante at Verona, and other Poems," and he occupied
himself also with the preparations for the volume of translations which in 1861 saw the light under the title, " The
Early Italian Poets, from Ciullo D'Alcano to Dante Alighieri," and was subsequently reprinted as " Dante and

his Cycle." At the close of the earlier edition of this work, indeed, "Dante at Verona" is announced as shortly to be published. This volume never saw the light. The poems, however, which were intended for it, and found subsequently a place in the collection of 1870, were principally written before 1861. The dates of most of these are conjectural, and some even which, like "Jenny," were begun early, were not perfected until late. Practically, however, "My Sister's Sleep" and "The Blessed Damozel" represent what he regarded as his earliest accomplishment, and practically, also, these works belong to the frame of mind as well as the period in which he painted The Girlhood of Mary Virgin. Between the execution of the painting and that of the poems there is no comparison. The mystical adoration of Mediævalism is finely shown in this, Rossetti's first exhibited picture. The face of the Virgin who is embroidering the Annunciation lily, which a young angel is tending, is carefully painted from his sister Christina; St. Anna, who is on the right of the Virgin, being taken from Mrs. Rossetti. The details are elaborate, and much of the painting is admirable. Scarcely a trace, however, is there of the marvellous colouring which, so far as regards execution, became the most striking characteristic of Rossetti's painting, and the drawing, which was never Rossetti's strong point, is weak and uncertain. As the creation of a youth of twenty, it is remarkable, and its imaginative gifts entitle it to its place beside the works of Rossetti's two associates in setting forth the gospel of Pre-Raphaelitism. It is signed Dante Gabriele Rossetti, P.R.B. In the case of the poem, "The Blessed Damozel," however, no excuse for immaturity or shortcoming has to be made. In place of promise there is performance.

Though imaginative in conception, in the sense that no known or recorded event supplied the basis, "My Sister's Sleep" is a purely domestic poem. It is full of pathos, and, like much of Rossetti's poetical work, a little "set" or elaborate. The movements of the characters are described with a fulness of detail which explains why, in some estimates, the poem is held to be Pre-Raphaelite. It is, indeed, characteristic of the school to introduce into a simple story of death and life a verse such as that descriptive of how

> " Our mother rose from where she sat :
>   Her needles, as she laid them down,
>   Met lightly, and her silken gown
> Settled : no other noise than that."

And the curiously mystical and uncanny description of the heavens, as seen through the window, is like the background of a picture. This stanza is quoted as it appears in the collection of 1870, and not as it was first written—

> " Without, there was a cold moon up,
>   Of winter radiance sheer and thin ;
>   The hollow halo it was in
> Was like an icy crystal cup."

Though not the first to use this metre, Rossetti was desirous that the fact should be known that "My Sister's Sleep" was earlier in date than the publication of Tennyson's " In Memoriam," in which the same stanza is adopted. It furnishes a curious comment upon the individuality with which a poet can charge the very forms he employs, that the notion of resemblance between the metre of this poem and that of "In Memoriam" is scarcely suggested.

"The Blessed Damozel" is a far more ambitious and successful effort. So few were the readers of *The Germ,* that the poem remained practically unknown. Passages from it were, however, quoted by those who had read it in print or in manuscript, or, it may be, had heard it recited, and thus served to keep up a sort of mystery eminently suited to the work. Apart altogether from the question of the poet's age when it was written, it is the most remarkable poem of its day. Unlike some of the works by which it was followed, which owed something, at least, though never much, to the influence of writers under whose ascendency Rossetti had come for a time, this poem seems to have no literary prototype. Nothing in it is directly assignable to the influence of the early reading of Shakespeare, Byron, or Scott, the subsequent influence of Keats, or that of the closely-studied Dante. Such inspiration as is traceable to any source whatever belongs assumably to the pictures of those early Italian painters, whom Rossetti had lovingly studied, and to domestic influences to which he yielded. Those who are acquainted with the beauty and purity of life of his mother and sisters, and their devotional tendencies, know how much in his early work, with its mystic piety, drew its inspiration thence.

Essentially a painter's poem, "The Blessed Damozel" surprises by its imaginative pictures of the unknown

world.   In the spirit of Milton, rather than in that or
Dante, Rossetti may claim to have "presumed into the
Heav'n of Heav'ns"—

> "An earthly guest and drawn empyreal air."

Nothing in the descriptions recalls any preceding work.
In Protestant literature, at least, it is a thing unheard
of in a poem in a sense religious, to find no trace
of the biblical phraseology, the influences of which
on much that is noblest in the English language
cannot easily be over-estimated.   Rossetti knew the
English Bible well, but seems to have drawn little
from it.   His style has more that reminds one of the
Vulgate, into which he used to dip.   The language of
this, especially in the Psalms and Lamentations, has a
beauty of its own to which no scholar can be insensible,
and a richness of phrase by which Rossetti was likely to
be captivated.   The use of the word gold to describe the
bar on which the blessed Damozel leans is almost the
only conventional expression in the poem.   An image
with which the second stanza concludes—

> "Her hair that lay along her back
> Was yellow like ripe corn,"

may have been suggested by Musset's "Chanson de For-
tunio," a poem, in its way, as perfect as "The Blessed
Damozel," and written a dozen years earlier, in which the
poet asserts of the heroine—

> "Qu'elle est blonde
> Comme les blés."

The representation of the spectacle to be contemplated

from "the rampart of God's house," so high "she scarce
can see the sun," is marvellously daring and original—

> " It lies in Heaven, across the flood
>   Of ether, as a bridge.
> Beneath, the tides of day and night
>   With flame and darkness ridge
> The void, as low as where this earth
>   Spins like a fretful midge."

The boldness, almost amounting to grotesqueness, of the
last simile is remarkable. The illustration is, however,
well calculated to serve its purpose. Equally startling is
a second illustration, a few stanzas further on, when it is
said—

> " The sun was gone now ; the curled moon
>   Was like a little feather
> Fluttering far down the gulf."

A precedent for this kind of daring may be found in
"Festus," by Mr. Philip James Bailey, in which Rossetti,
with all cultivated men of his epoch, took great delight.
Rossetti's work has, however, nothing except courage in
common with "Festus," a poem to the beauties of which
the younger generation shows itself little sensible, but
which exercised in its day an influence the extent of
which is even now scarcely recognized. The picture of
the fair saint conveyed in the opening stanzas of "The
Blessed Damozel" is worthy of Keats, and seems wrought
in a species of ecstasy, while the manner in which the
leavening influence of human emotion is shown, even in
the mansions of the blest, is, in its way, unique. As an
imaginative conception, and as an illustration of the
power of mystic insight possessed by Rossetti, the

entire poem has highest interest. Other poems, of the same or a subsequent epoch, have similar gifts. It is like a lesson in Rossetti's method to see how lovely in themselves, and how picturesque are the words employed, and how the remote significations of scenes are sought rather than their obvious meanings.

In " Love's Nocturn " the stanza—

> " Where in groves the gracile Spring
> 　　Trembles, with mute orison
> Confidently strengthening,
> 　　Water's voice and wind's as one
> 　Shed an echo in the sun.
> 　　　Soft as Spring,
> Master, bid it sing and moan."

Here "gracile," a word with the introduction of which into English Rossetti may be credited, combines delightfully the ideas, gracious and fragile. " Mute orison " is, again, an eminently poetical combination. It may be doubted, however, whether from the stanza, with or without the context, many readers get a very distinct idea. This poem is, indeed, full of happiest epithet, and abounds with descriptive passages, such as that already quoted, at once lovely and nebulous. Such is, to furnish another instance, the account of Dreamland—

> " Vaporous, unaccountable,
> 　Dreamland lies forlorn of light,
> 　Hollow, like a breathing shell."

It may here be urged that the subject itself is incapable of close definition, and that the words are purposely chosen to convey this idea. Accepting this view, even, the fact remains that in the early poems of this epoch the phrases are often more beautiful than interpretative. Where they are happiest and most significant it is rather in descriptions of the broader effects of nature, in pictures of celestial phenomena and other objects open to the dwellers in towns than in close observations of nature's secrets. Rossetti, as will be seen, lived during no inconsiderable portion of his life in the country, and was sensible to its beauties. His was, however, to a great extent, a town life.

The change in mind indicated by the passage from "The Blessed Damozel " to "Sister Helen," was ascribable in part to the changed conditions of his life, involving, as a natural and healthy consequence, his being left to his own devices. During his intercourse with Hunt and Millais, his was the most imaginative, as well as the most richly stored, mind. Neither of these associates of his youth will dispute the obligation he was under to Rossetti for suggestions of subject, and for general poetical illumination. At the same time, a corresponding influence was exercised upon Rossetti by his two friends, and especially by Mr. Hunt, whose earnestness and concentration were well calculated to impress and influence his associate. Perhaps the most striking fact in connection with Rossetti's life-work is the commencement of the great unfinished picture, Found. In this work, which, though later by a year or two than the composition of "Sister Helen," belongs to the same period of intellectual development, Rossetti strove to be faithful to influences which had passed or were passing out of his life. Bent on showing his power to deal with a subject drawn from modern life, and to demonstrate the dramatic quality which had developed itself in his mind, he still at the outset adhered in his workmanship to his early method.

The picture, which has more than once been described, presents an unhappy girl who has been sacrificed to the insatiable lust of the great city, and who cowering against the wall of a graveyard is recognized by a rustic lover, who, while the wan light of early morning is struggling with the fading glare of the gas, is driving into London a cart in which is a white calf. The face of the woman, partly hidden by her dishevelled hair and the calf, are painted upon Pre-Raphaelite principles; the remainder of the work, so far as it is finished, is different in workmanship.

Whatever may be the opinion as to the relative value of the two methods, it seems that the romantic style is that in which Rossetti moves most at his ease. It is the direct outcome of his mind so soon as he gets free from the sustained influence of the distinguished painter whose studio he shared. In poetry, however, and as has been said in painting, in the latter especially, in subsequent years the tendency to mysticism asserted itself. Found, however, marks clearly the period when what, for want of an adequate word, may be called Rossetti-ism, establishes itself over previous influences.

To the books which he studied may be added "The Death of Marlowe," by Richard Hengist Horne ; Sir Henry Taylor's plays which he greatly admired ; and the "Gesta Romanorum," which he read in a translation, and with the crude stories in which, at least as subjects for poems and pictures, he expresses himself disappointed. Many other works in which he delighted might be mentioned, including the poems of that powerful and erratic genius Thomas Lovell Beddoes. Ballad and romance literature remained however, if not the chief, at least the most easily and advantageously assimilated food. That Rossetti was ever a close student of the Elizabethan drama does not appear. Shakespeare he studied from boyhood ; Marlowe was an early favourite ; of Chapman, either as a translator or as a dramatist, he knew little ; and Webster's two great tragedies came within his ken. As a whole, however, the literature which has been prodigal of delights to most men of imaginative powers or tendencies, influenced him but little. In the depreciated " Gesta Romanorum " he found the materials for " The Staff and Scrip," a poem which also belongs in part to the mystical period, and was projected not later than 1849. An admirable illustration of Rossetti's method is afforded by a comparison of this poem with the story as it appears in the original. In the early English translation, edited by Sir Frederick Madden for the Roxburgh Club, the tale is called " The Bloody Shirt : of a Knight who restored a Princess to her Kingdom, and of her gratitude to him " [Harl. MS. 7333]. The Emperor Fredrericus *(sic)* of Rome bequeaths on his death-bed his entire empire to his daughter. " So what time that a certayne Erle hurde of this, after the deth of the Emperour, he come to the dameselle and stered hire to synne, and anoon the dameselle enclined to his wordis. So whanne the dameselle was filid (defiled) with synne, he put hire out of hire empire ; and than she made lamentacion more than ony man can trowe, and gede (went) into an other kyngdome or cuntre." Sitting in her sorrow she receives the visit of a "faire yong knyghte, sitting vp on a faire hors," who asking the cause of her grief receives the full history. On the promise that she will be his love he undertakes to recover her heritage. Before setting out to do this he imposes conditions : "If it happe me to dye for the (thee) in batill, and not to have victory, that thou sette out my blody serke (shirt) on a perch afore, for twey skilis (two reasons) ; the first is that the sighte of my serke may meve (move) the to wepe as ofte tyme as thou lokist theron ; The secunde skile (reason) is, for I woll, that whenne ony man comyth to the, for to haue the for wife, that thou renne (run) to the serke, and biholde the serke and sey to thiself, 'God forbede that euer I sholde take ony to my husbond, after the deth of this lord, which deyde for my love and recoveryd myne heritage.' " According to his foreboding the lover won the victory and regained her estates, but "gate his deth " in so doing. His shirt soaked in his life's blood was brought to the lady, and when she saw it " all her bowelis (bowels) weere troubelyd more than tunge may telle." The conditions, it is needless to say, were observed, and when suitors came she rushed into the chamber and with a "lamentabill voys" cried out according to his suggestion. "And so she answerid to all that come to hire for that erende, and fayr endid hire lyfe."

Like the stories of the Arthurian cycle, this legend breathes the very spirit of chivalry, and in the primitive language in which it is couched has a certain quaint pathos and nobility. A bargain, such as the knight made, was quite according to the rules of chivalry, and the lady whose fair life ended in eternal devotion to his memory, as signalized in the grim souvenir would not be held unhappy among women. In substituting for the bloody shirt the staff and scrip of a pilgrim returning from Palestine, Rossetti seems false to the sincerity of his ordinary workmanship. The name of Queen Blanchelys which he bestows on the heroine, and that of Duke Luke assigned her oppressor, are entirely happy. Quite in the spirit of " The Blessed Damozel" is the description of the queen as she is first seen by the pilgrim.

> " The Queen sat idle by her loom :
>   She heard the arras stir,
> And looked up sadly : through the room
>   *The sweetness sickened her*
>   *Of musk and myrrh.*
>
> Her women, standing two and two,
>   In silence combed the fleece.
> The pilgrim said, ' Peace be with you,
>   Lady ; ' and bent his knees.
>   She answered, ' Peace.'
>
> Her eyes were like the wave within ;
>   Like water-reeds the poise
> Of her soft body, dainty thin ;
>   And like the water's noise
>   Her plaintive voice."

The lines in italics in the first stanza are in keeping with Pre-Raphaelite execution ; the last stanza anticipates many descriptive passages to be found in subsequent poems by Mr. Swinburne and Mr. Morris.

The pilgrim departs armed by her with a sharp sword whose blade " he kissed," feeling the while its belt about his body, as sweet as her own arms, a green banner with "one white lily stem," and a white shield on which he emblazons her face. He returns victorious with the sword broken in his hand, the battered shield by his side, and the banner across his lifeless face. She keeps the staff and scrip, which he has left with one of her handmaidens to be given her in case of his death, and is faithful to his memory until life ends, when the poet transfers the lovers to heaven, where the action is finished. Addressing the warrior he says—

> " The lists are set in Heaven to-day,
> The bright pavilions shine ;
> Fair hangs thy shield, and none gainsay ;
> The trumpets sound in sign
> That she is thine."

The blending of human devotion with pious mysticism is eminently characteristic of Rossetti's early productions. Something of the kind indeed permeated most of his works. Though an adherent of no creed Rossetti possessed a mind of eminently devotional tendencies. "The Staff and Scrip" is moreover stiff with elaborate embroidery. Few of Rossetti's poems have the light agile motion of unimpeded youth. Stateliness and splendour are his. The virgin moves with long, heavy draperies, with serene look, and with the aureole around her head. His heroines wear almost always some nimbus of sorrow, of fate, or of death.

In July in the year 1853 Rossetti made one of his few excursions, visiting Mr. William Bell Scott, in Newcastle-on-Tyne. In company with his host he went to Carlisle and Hexham, with both of which he was delighted. Returning to Chatham Place, where he is again found in August of the same year, he visited many places of interest in the Western Midlands—Coventry, Warwick, Kenilworth, &c. From Kenilworth he walked to Stratford. To the beginning of the following year belongs the death of Deverell, by which Rossetti was greatly affected. At this period he speaks of himself and his companions, in terms probably of banter, as " too transcendent spirits far in advance of the age." He is desirous not to parade pecuniary difficulties in the face of strangers, and is anxious that the matters whereof he was accustomed to write should not be mentioned in the presence of friends so intimate even as James Hannay, who appears at this time to have been a frequent guest. A conscientious worker, he hesitates about making additions to paintings for which he had commissions for fear that by doing uncovenanted for and unpaid for work he should get the character of being enthusiastic.

In painting, meanwhile, the growth of the romantic and dramatic style is less easily traced, inasmuch as this is curiously blended with the mystical.

In a series of monographs of distinguished or representative writers, it is out of place to dwell at any length upon pictorial works, with which indeed the present writer confesses his inability to deal. It is only accordingly as they illustrate the intellectual growth which is traceable in his writings that Rossetti's pictures are mentioned. In the works which followed The Girlhood of Mary Virgin, Rossetti is seen affirming his strength by sustained exertion under the influence of Mr.

Holman Hunt and Mr. Ford Madox Brown, and, even in a less degree, of Sir John Millais.

In The Laboratory, a work illustrative of a poem. of Mr. Browning, and in Michael Scott's Wooing, the mysticism which is paramount in The Girlhood of Mary Virgin and the Ecce Ancilla Domini, and has been held by Mr. F. G. Stephens, Rossetti's subtlest critic, to have found its highest development, in " The Blessed Damozel " both poem and picture, the Bride, and Astarte Syriaca, is combatted by the romantic. The Parable of Love, an unimportant drawing given to Mr. Coventry Patmore, Mr. Stephens takes as the prototype of the mystic designs of Rossetti. The Laboratory is the prototype of the studies of human passion, of the pictures which deal less with contemplation than with action in which perhaps the highest outcome of Rossetti is found. As The Laboratory belongs to 1849, it follows that the mystical, which many years later was to resume its sway in painting, was combatted by the romantic earlier, in regard to pictures, than, so far as is known, it was in poetry. Another painting, founded like The Laboratory upon Mr. Browning's poem, which Rossetti with his bell-like utterance was fond of reading aloud, is Kate the Queen, from " Pippa Passes." This, supposed by Mr. Sharp to be lost, was exhibited at the Burlington Club. It is a finished oil sketch for a large picture never completed.

CHAPTER VII.

DURING his residence in Chatham Place Rossetti came under the most potent influence of his life. The most romantic and touching episode in his career is found in his courtship, marriage, and early bereavement, and in the sacrifice by which the last event was followed. Concerning the long engagement, and the brief nuptials, few particulars are preserved. Both are passed over by his biographers with slight comment. From his letters to Mr. Ford Madox Brown, however, who next to his brother, and in some respects even more than his brother, was his most trusted friend and counsellor, and from his correspondence with his family it is possible to frame an idea of this connection, the influence of which upon his work, during some of the most productive years of his life, cannot easily be overestimated. Somewhere near 1850 his friend Deverell met Miss Elizabeth Eleanor Siddall, and was so struck with her beauty of face and form that he persuaded her to sit to him. She was the daughter of a Sheffield tradesman, and was occupied in London as a milliner's assistant. Sharing his friend's enthusiasm, Rossetti, towards the close of 1850 or beginning of 1851, induced her to sit to him also. She had not long been with him before he recognized in her a strong aptitude for art. This, with characteristic zeal, he sought to foster, and the position of model was soon associated with that of student. Under Rossetti's zealous tuition her progress was rapid, and her water-colour drawings soon displayed marked proficiency, and a fine sense of colour. By the keen stimulus of the admiration she excited, her faculties generally were quickened, and her achievements in poetry were no less remarkable than those in painting.

A result all but inevitable, when to the attractions of youth and beauty is added the magnetism that springs from kindred tastes and occupations, ensued. The close intimacy involved in the relationship of master and pupil gave every opportunity for successful wooing, and Miss Siddall became affianced to her teacher. Apart from her intellectual gifts, she was at that time peculiarly calculated to stimulate the imagination and fix the fancy of a painter. A portrait of her head painted by herself two or three years later—it is signed E. E. S., and dated 1853–54—is in the possession of Mr. William Michael Rossetti. It is admirably painted, and not in the least idealized. Full justice is, however, done to the beauty of the face, the dreaming, abstracted look in which, due in part to suffering, is well caught ; the long oval of the cheek, the clearly cut features, the pale luminous complexion, the mouth with that special curve of lip which artists have always affected, the large drooping eyes and full eyebrows, are shown. Her hair, of a deep bronzed red, is parted in the middle, and its thick wiry folds are gathered in a mass suggesting the use of the net—then a customary portion of female head-gear ;—no net is, however, em-

ployed. In the delicate set of the head upon the neck
is found the only indication of her figure, which was tall
and eminently graceful.

The exact date of the engagement between Rossetti and
Miss Siddall cannot be fixed. It was probably 1853 ;
certainly not later than 1854. At Miss Siddall's request
the contract was kept secret, and its first publication to
Rossetti's close friends seems to have been contrary to
her wishes. Those, however, with whom Rossetti lived
on terms of intimacy can have had little doubt as to
the nature of the feeling on one side at least. Rossetti's
correspondence at this date—most of it as yet unpublished
—is full of affectionate references to Miss Siddall. To
Mr. Madox Brown he speaks of her invariably as Lizzie,
coupling frequently with the appellation some endearing
adjective, and using at times such names, caressing or
grotesque, as secure affection loves to bestow. So
early as August 25, 1853, he communicates the intelli-
gence that Liz is going to begin a picture for the Royal
Academy. The following year he tells of her introduction to his sister Christina, and to William and Mary
Howitt. Writing to his mother he speaks of Lizzie and
himself scratching their initials on a stone at Old Roar.
On the 23rd May, a day which, somewhat curiously, was
to be that of his subsequent wedding, he indulges, to Mr.
Madox Brown in all a lover's ecstasies. Writing from
5, High Street, Hastings, he says : " Lizzie is looking
lovelier than ever," and later on, " Every one adores and
reveres Lizzie. I made sketches of her with iris stuck in
her dear hair the other day, and we all wrote up our
monograms on the panel of the window in memorial of

the very pleasant day we had spent at the farm." The farm was a house belonging to Miss Barbara Leigh Smith, subsequently Mrs. Bodichon, some miles from Hastings, which Rossetti more than once visited. Such outbursts of admiration on the part of Rossetti were not uncommon, and at times involved some trouble to his friends. At the period when a planned excursion was on the point of being carried out, or an immediate return from one was expedient, the lover, seeing his mistress in some pose of exceptional beauty, would insist upon everything being suspended until he had taken a sketch. Later on in the communication from which the last quotation was taken, he continues—" I think I told you that she and I are going to illustrate the old Scottish ballads which Allingham is editing for Routledge. She has just done her first block (from ' Clerk Saunders '), and it is lovely. Her power of designing even increases greatly, and her fecundity of invention and facility are quite wonderful, much greater than mine." In April, 1855, she spends with him a day at Ruskin's, and he states with delight that R(uskin) thought her a noble woman. His happiness at this time appears to have been exuberant, though damped somewhat by pecuniary difficulties, and by constant anxiety for her health, for which there was indeed but too much cause. His letters are full of a species of banter to which he was always given, but of the existence of which outsiders have scarcely dreamt. At times he writes in rhyme, not poetry, but pure, jubilant, light-hearted doggerell, redolent of hope and excitement. In another mood he is wild with apprehension. In March, 1854, Dr. Garth Wilkinson, an eminent homœopathic physician, is called in, and declares Miss Siddall to have curvature of the spine. All the consolation the lover can find is that the case, though pronounced serious, is not hopeless.

In February, 1857, the engagement is openly mentioned, though even then its promulgation is opposed by Miss Siddall. References to her at this time are constant, and in presence of contemplated nuptials some attempt is even made at economy of expenditure—at all times a difficult task for Rossetti. The idea of purchasing a coveted Hogarth is abandoned, the young painter taking an example from his correspondent, Mr. Ford Madox Brown, and dismissing all idea of the treasure as " a luxury he can't afford." In April, 1860, when the marriage is imminent, a severe attack of illness on the part of Miss Siddall throws him once more into extreme apprehension. On the 17th of April he writes from 12, East Parade, Hastings, to his brother, in language of extreme anxiety, saying that if he were to lose her he does not know what effect it might have upon his mind. He has, he states, been inquiring after a special license since he has fears of her ability to stand the cold of the church. With so much delay and expense, however, will this be attended, he hardly sees how it is possible to obtain it. The ordinary license he has, and he trusts to God he may be able to use it, adding once more, " If not . . . I do not know how it might end for me." He urges his brother not to dwell in his letters upon the state of her health as " it is so wretched a subject, especially at such a moment." On the 11th of the following month (May) he writes from Hastings to say that to-morrow, his birth-

day, has been fixed for his marriage, but Lizzie is too ill.
Not long deferred was the event, since on the 23rd of
the same month he writes to Mr. Madox Brown : " All
hail from Lizzie and myself, just back from church."

The ceremony was performed in St. Clement's Church,
Hastings, the officiating clergyman being the Rev. T.
Nightingale.   In the announcement which Rossetti
sent to his brother for insertion in *The Times* he
describes himself as Dante Gabriel, eldest son of the
late Gabriel Rossetti, of Vasto degli Abruzzi, Kingdom
of Naples, and speaks of his wife as " Elizabeth Eleanor,
daughter of the late Charles Siddall, of Sheffield."   The
married couple then went to Paris by way of Folkestone
and Boulogne, staying in the latter town some days.
Here he sees a chateau "with a wonderful garden and
many paintable things, and has an idea of taking it
unless they find it advisable to push for the South."   In
Paris he stays at the Hôtel Meurice until he finds it
expedient, still under the spell of economy, to get into
cheaper lodgings.

Between the apprehensions for the health of his wife,
and the feeling that it is time he returns to work and earns
some money, he is a little perplexed even in the very
month of honey.   The chief duty to art which he per-
forms while in Paris is having several good looks at " the
great Paul Veronese, the greatest picture in the world,
beyond a doubt."

After this trip Rossetti returned with his bride to 14,
Chatham Place, at which house considerable alterations
had been made in anticipation of their arrival.

Between the first meeting of Rossetti and Miss Siddall

and his bringing her home as his wife a delay of nearly a decade had taken place. This was to some extent attributable to prudential motives. With an uncertain income Rossetti did not dare to face the responsibilities of marriage. One more passage on this subject from a correspondence, the right to publish which is reserved for another, is all on which I shall venture. On the 5th March, 1861, Mr. Madox Brown is told that Lizzie has just had a dead baby. Particulars as to the attention she receives, and the anxiety she inspires, follow. A development of Mrs. Rossetti's illness, the root of which was consumption, consisted in neuralgia, relief from which could only be found in laudanum. To this seductive and dangerous agent Mrs. Rossetti trusted, with the result that she took an overdose. One night in 1862 the Madox Browns, then living on Highgate Rise, were alarmed by a violent knocking at the door. This was due to Rossetti, who, after frantically seeking one physician after another, aroused his friend to aid him in his extreme emergency. All was, however, in vain. The spirit had fled ; the fair frame was tenantless, and she whom Rossetti in sustained adoration had just painted as Regina Cordium, had passed away for ever from his life.

How poignant and enduring was the grief of Rossetti, is now a matter of history. Though mention of her name fades from his correspondence, the devotion of the lover is shown in his work after her death as before. Among the many portraits of her in her own person, or in his imaginative work, which exist, none is more faithful as a portrait, nor more interesting as a record, than the lovely Beata Beatrix, painted the year following her death and bought by Lord Mount-Temple. Of this work he executed a small replica in water-colours in 1871, and a second in oil the following year. A third replica in oil, painted in 1880, is one of the last works he lived to finish ; how abiding was his affection is thus shown. The scene which followed her death is known. On the day of the funeral Rossetti walked into the chamber in which the body lay. In his hand was a book into which, at her bidding, he had copied his poems. Regardless of those present he spoke to her as though she were still living, telling her that the poems were written to her and were hers, and that she must take them with her. He then placed the volume beside her face in the coffin, leaving it to be buried with her in Highgate Cemetery. This touching scene will some day doubtless be the subject of a picture. Time, after its wont, hallowed and sanctified the memory of loss, but the bereavement was long and keenly felt. Meanwhile, the entombment of Rossetti's poems had an effect upon which the writer had not calculated. They were familiar to many friends, and passages of them were retained in the recollection of some. These poems were during subsequent years the subject of much anxiety and wonderment, and the existence of the buried treasure was mentioned with reverence and sympathy, and with something of awe. Seven years later Rossetti, upon whom pressure to permit the exhumation of the volume had constantly been put, gave a reluctant consent. With the permission of the Home Secretary the coffin was opened by a friend of Rossetti and the volume was withdrawn. Its contents were copied by the author and by Mr. Fairfax Murray, and were ultimately printed in the first collection of poems. A portion of them only was new. Some had been printed in *The Germ* and *The Oxford and Cambridge Magazine*, and others were in the possession of friends. Of many of them, however, no memory existed, and these, without the extorted permission to open the grave, must have been entirely lost.

CHAPTER VIII.

CONSIDERATION of the poems making up the volume known as the first collection belongs to a later epoch in Rossetti's life. One or two of them have already been discussed, and many of them, perhaps the majority, were written during the happy period of courtship and the brief honeymoon of wedded life. One even bears strongly upon what has previously been said as to the wooing and espousal. The poem entitled "The Portrait," though written in 1847 with no reference to any actual fact, was touched up after the death of Mrs. Rossetti. It is easy to fancy he alludes to her picture when he writes—

> " I gaze until she seems to stir,—
>   Until mine eyes almost aver
>   That now, even now, the sweet lips part
>   To breathe the words of the sweet heart :—
>   And yet the earth is over her."

A little further in the poem he continues—

> " In painting her I shrined her face
>   'Mid mystic trees, where light falls in
>   Hardly at all.
>   *   *   *   *

A deep, dim wood ; and there she stands
　As in that wood that day ; for so
Was the still movement of her hands,
　And such the pure lines gracious flow ;
And passing fair the type must seem,
Unknown the presence and the dream.
　'Tis she : though of herself, alas !
　Less than her shadow on the grass,
Or than her image in the stream."

One more stanza serves to present the scene in which the portrait was executed, and seems to hint at the spot where the incident occurred—

" But when that hour my soul won strength,
　For words whose silence wastes and kills,
Dull raindrops smote us, and at length
　Thundered the heat within the hills.
That eve I spoke those words again,
Beside the pelted window-pane ;
　And there she hearkened what I said,
　With under-glances that surveyed
The empty pastures blind with rain."

This description, equally noteworthy for tenderness, and for the elaborateness of detail which is characteristic of much of Rossetti's work, suggesting that there was a divided individuality, half of which scrutinized and studied, while the other half felt, might, it almost seems, be assigned to April, 1854, when Rossetti had followed Miss Siddall to Hastings, whither, on account of illness, she had been sent. Its scene would in that case be the farmhouse near Hastings, belonging to Miss Barbara Leigh Smith, to which previous reference has been made. The assumption is necessarily conjectural. In his correspondence, however, with Mr. Ford Madox Brown, Rossetti describes himself painting her portrait, refers to the shelter from the rain, and dwells upon their carving their monograms on the panel of a window, in memory of an exceptionally happy day. In the case of a poem which seems directly inspired by personal feeling, an attempt to fix a time and locality, even if not wholly conclusive, may be pardoned.

To this happy period belongs a piece of prose descriptive of nature, which has not yet been published. Writing from Hastings, still in 1854, in a period of Lotos eating, pleasant to reflect upon, he says, "I lie often on the cliffs which are lazy themselves, all grown with grass and herbage, not athletic, as at Dover, nor gaunt, as at North Shields. Through the summer mists the sea and sky are one, and, if you half shut your eyes, as of course you do, there is no swearing to the distant sail as boat or bird, while just under one's feet the near boats stand together immoveable, as if their shadows clogged them, and they would not come in after all, but loved to see the land. So one may lie, and symbolize till one goes to sleep, and that be a symbol, too, perhaps."

A literary work the completion of which belongs to the period of courtship and wedded life, is the "Early Italian Poets, from Ciullo d'Alcamo to Dante Alighieri (1100–1200–1300,") with the "Vita Nuova" of Dante, which was published in 1861, with a dedication, signed D. G. R. : "Whatever is mine in this book is inscribed to my wife." The inception of this work belongs of course to the outset of Rossetti's career, when he was living in his father's house, and listening to endless disquisitions upon the works and meaning of Dante and the poets of his cycle. Most of the translations, moreover, must rank among his earliest productions. They began in 1846, or even 1845, and nine-tenths of them were probably finished by the end of 1848 or beginning of 1849.

Dante's "Vita Nuova" is of course, a classic, and a work which may well arrest the attention of scholars. It had in part, so early as 1835, been translated by Rossetti's godfather, Charles Lyell, and a full translation by Mr. (now Sir Theodore) Martin trod close on the heels of that of Rossetti. Italian, moreover—even the Italian of the thirteenth and fourteenth centuries—offered little difficulty to Rossetti, who also delighted in the exercise of intellect involved in the search after rhyming equivalents in English to a language offering such facilities for versification as the Italian. Making all allowances, however, it remains doubtful whether any but a lover so exceptionally endowed as Rossetti, and so enamoured of womanhood as to be able to assign to a mistress, real or imagined ; raptures, sincere or artificial, with which he might be called upon to deal, would have had the patience to translate the whole work.

Ciullo d'Alcamo, who is earliest of all, since his writings date back to 1172–78, is all well enough. In his dialogue between a lover and his lady beats a full pulse of human passion. The lady appears, it is true, needlessly coy and inaccessible. Her coldness is, how-ever, but simulated, worn apparently for the sake of inciting her lover to further raptures. Her heart listens with scarcely concealed delight to his wooing, and she is glad of an excuse that shall justify him in continuing to

flatter and to plead.   Portions of this poem have, moreover, a faint perfume of the garden scene in Romeo and
Juliet.   Juliet, were she given to banter, and had her
secret not been surprised "ere " she "was ware ," might
warn her lover in some such language as this—

> " Nay, though my heart were prone to love,
>   I would not grant it leave.
> Hark ! should my father or his kin
>   But find thee here this eve,
> Thy loving body and lost breath,
>   Our moat might well receive.
> Whatever path to come here thou dost know,
> By the same path I counsel thee to go."

And his answer, though unlike anything assigned to
Romeo, is not dissimilar in spirit—

> " Would'st thou in very truth that I
>   Were slain, and for thy sake ?
> Then let them hew me to such mince
>   As a man's limbs may make !
> But meanwhile I shall not stir hence,
>   Till of that fruit I take
> Which thou hast in thy garden, ripe enough :
> All day and night I thirst to think thereof."

Much of what follows is, however, difficult to any except
those "that be lovers."   Rossetti himself speaks in his
preface of the imperfections of poems belonging to the
first epoch of Italian poetry, which, he says, are not all
to be charged to the translator.   Among these he classes
"its limited range of subjects and continual obscurity, as
well as its monotony in the use of rhyme, or frequent

substitution of assonances." Their beauties are, he
insists, of a kind that "can never again exist in art," and
they " offer, besides, a treasure of grace and variety in
the formation of their metres." This, doubtless, is true,
and the light which is cast upon certain forms of social
existence in mediæval Italy is also of signal value. The
monotony of subject of which complaint is made would,
however, except in the case of a man passionately
enamoured of womanhood, constitute a virtual prohibi-
tion of translation, and is an impediment even to their
perusal. It may safely be assumed that the translation
is complete and final. A man with a mind more in accord
with what is mystic and transcendental in these poems
than Rossetti possessed is not often to be encountered.
When to this requirement are added a metrical power
and a command of rhyme altogether exceptional, an
irrepressible enthusiasm for the subject, and a keen
sympathy with what is individual in many of the
utterances, gifts all of which Rossetti possessed, a combination of essentials not likely to be found again in
another man is offered.

The translations are said to be close ; they are certainly
terse and vigorous. To those unacquainted, as are
necessarily most English readers, with the originals, which
are not too easily accessible, the conquest of difficulty
achieved by Rossetti is not immediately apparent. His
task was nothing less than finding in a language, which
with all its merits, including its fitness for the highest
poetical expression, is yet hard and unyielding, equivalents for the amorous phrases and redundant rhymes
of the most plastic and musical of tongues. Rossetti's

success in this effort is remarkable. Few of the poems read like translations, and the use of such devices employed by Rossetti in his original poems, as the rhyme on a syllable not ordinarily accented, as when "sob-broken" does duty as a rhyme to "then," and "sing" rhymes to "sorrowing," add to the feeling that the poems are charged with his own personality. Seldom indeed has a poet been able to get more thoroughly inside the works of other men, and the book in this, as in some other respects, stands almost, if not quite, alone in literature. Rossetti is, perhaps, most at his ease in his translations from the "Vita Nuova," and from Guido Cavalcanti, who is a special favourite with him. In the sonnets the triumph over difficulty is the more remarkable; the poetical qualities are perhaps better seen in the rendering of *ballata* or *canzone*. A single illustration of this may suffice. The most remarkable sonnet in the volume is that of Cavalcanti, in which Dante is rebuked for the way of life into which he fell after the death of Beatrice. The occasion of the sonnet is probably, as the translator points out, the same infirmity for which Dante makes Beatrice rebuke him in the lines in the thirtieth canto of " Il Purgatorio," commencing—

> " Quando di carne a spirto era salita
> E bellezza e virtù cresciuta m'era
> Fu' io a lui men cara e men gradita."

> " I come to thee by day-time constantly,
> But in thy thoughts too much of baseness find :
> Greatly it grieves me for thy gentle mind,
> And for thy many virtues gone from thee.

It was thy wont to shun much company
    Unto all sorry concourse ill inclined :
    And still thy speech of me, heartfelt and kind,
Had made me treasure up thy poetry.
But now I dare not, for thine abject life,
    Make manifest that I approve thy rhymes ;
        Nor come I in such sort that thou may'st know.
    Ah ! prythee read this sonnet many times :
So shall that evil one who bred this strife,
        Be thrust from thy dishonour'd soul and go."

Apart from the interest this possesses as a record, unimpeachable in authority, of such shortcoming on the part of Dante as brings him within the ken of ordinary mortals, and takes from him a portion of the awe, as well as of the extreme veneration, with which men are inclined to regard the great light of mediæval literature, it is a fine sonnet. On the page immediately opposite is a rendering of a *ballata* of the same author. Six or eight lines of this are sufficient to illustrate the opinion advanced —

    " Within a copse I met a shepherd maid,
        More fair, I said, than any star to see.
      She came with waving tresses pale and bright,
        With rosy cheek, and loving eyes of flame,
      Guiding the lambs beneath her wand aright,
        Her naked feet still had the dew on them,
        As, singing like a lover, so she came,
      Joyful, and fashioned for all ecstasy.

It is impossible not to feel the free motion of this, its soft, untrammelled, unconventional grace.

A special merit in these translations is the selection of words which, without any character of antiquity, are full of archaic suggestion. Two opening stanzas of the lovely *canzone* to his " Dead Lady of Giacomino Pugliesi Knight of Prato," will illustrate this—

> " Death, why hast thou made life so hard to bear,
>   Taking my lady hence ?   Hast thou no whit
>   Of shame ?   The youngest flower and the. most fair
>   Thou hast pluck'd away, and the world wanteth it.
>   O leaden Death, hast thou no pitying?
>   Our warm loves' very spring
>   Thou stopp'st and endest what was holy and meet ;
>   And of my gladdening,
>   Mak'st a most woful thing,
>   And in my heart dost bid the bird not sing
>   That sang so sweet.
>
>   Once the great joy and solace that I had
>   Was more than is with other gentlemen :—
>   Now is my love gone hence, who made me glad.
>   With her that hope I lived in she hath ta'en,
>   And lett me nothing but these sighs and tears,—
>   Nothing of the old years
>   That come not back again,
>   Wherein I was so happy being hers ;
>   Now to mine eyes her face no more appears,
>   Nor doth her voice make music in mine ears,
>   As it did then."

In its continuance this poem remains equally beautiful and touching, and the manner in which the imaginary possessions mentioned by the poet as useless to bring back his dead love are described in English is a triumph of ingenuity and poetry. " The Early Italian Poets" secured the immediate recognition of scholars. Popular it could never be. An edition was slowly sold, and no long space before his death, Rossetti, while meditating a translation of the poems of Michael Angelo, turned to the work of his youth, rearranged its contents, changed its title, and issued a new edition, through his friend and publisher, Mr. Ellis.

The share of Mr. William Rossetti in lightening his brother's labours, in correcting proofs, in writing notes, and in collating the translation of the "Vita Nuova" with the original, finds full recognition in Rossetti's correspondence. In a letter to his brother he expresses his thanks for a most essential service, thoroughly performed. It is, indeed, obvious that but for the assistance rendered in this respect by this friend, staunch and helpful in all respects, the publication of the Italian Poets must have been deferred. Among the friends whom he consulted during the progress of the work were Mr. Coventry Patmore and Mr. William Allingham. A letter to the former, obligingly lent by him, sees now for the first time the light, and is interesting in many respects. It is, indeed, in some regards, a criticism by Rossetti upon his own performance. Unfortunately, like many of Rossetti's letters, it is undated, and does not even name the place whence it was despatched. It is simply headed "Wednesday night." Its probable date is 1853–4.

"DEAR PATMORE,—Before sending you the translations, I looked over Allingham's notes, and want to apprise you that all instances of varying metre, missing rhymes, &c., are close adherences to the originals, and not carelessnesses. He suggests rightly in one place that titles are wanted to the different poems—should any strike you in reading, I wish you'd jot them in the margin. I consider myself that descriptive headings—brief arguments—to the poems would, perhaps, be best, but leave all classification till the end. I can't say I always agree with A. or his preferences. For instance, there is one poem, at page 39, which he has not marked at all, and which seems to me almost the loveliest of the lot. I name this as occurring to me—but there are others. By the by, at page 156 is one copied out since I saw you, and which I think you'll agree with me in liking. It is by Cino da Pistoia (though generally attributed to Guido Guinicelli), and I believe it myself to be addressed to Dante on the occasion of the death of Beatrice. This is rather strengthened by Dante quoting it (though only in an argument on language) in his treatise ' De Vulgari Eloquio ; ' and there are various undoubted pieces of correspondence in rhyme (some I have translated, though not yet copied) between Cino and Dante.

"*Pray remember that all notes or suggested alterations of any kind whatever from you will be most thankfully received in the margin ;* especially suggestions as to any of the poems—if any—which you think the ones to be left out. With thanks beforehand for the trouble I'm thus saddling you with, and with a request for one line to tell of safe delivery of MSS.—when they reach you—believe me yours very sincerely,   D. G. Rossetti.

"P.S.—There are a good many more not yet copied, which you shall have in due course, if you care."

Other letters to Mr. Patmore, written from 45, Upper Albany Street, the house of Mr. William Rossetti and Mrs.

Rossetti, senior, contain some characteristically apprecia·
tive and cordial criticisms upon Mr. Patmore's own poems.

To this period of Rossetti's life belong his contributions
to *The Oxford and Cambridge Magazine*, a periodical
which, more fortunate than *The Germ*, contrived to live
through the year 1856. These poems are now obtainable
in other works, and the interest of the magazine is purely
bibliographical. It is, in fact, if less scarce at all, only
less scarce than *The Germ*. Rossetti's acceptance of an
engagement—it can scarcely be called a commission—to
take part in the decoration of the Union Debating Room
at Oxford took place in 1857. Though the result was, in
some respects, disaster, the influences of the visit to
Oxford and the friendships thus made was potent for
good.

Rossetti's share in the designs was due solely to his
love for art. Mr. Woodward, the architect of the University Museum at Oxford, was particularly desirous that the
details of the building, the capitals of the shafts, &c.,
should be left to the individual workman, who was to
work them out according to his own fancy. His instruc-
tions, however, were that the foliage chosen for conventional treatment should be that of the plants common in
the neighbourhood of Oxford. An idea of this kind was
eminently calculated to appeal to Rossetti, who took forth-
with keen interest in Mr. Woodward and his work, and
made occasional visits to Oxford to see how the scheme
progressed

In 1857 Mr. Woodward was about finishing the new
buildings for the Union Club in Oxford. Rossetti, who
accompanied him on a visit of inspection, was struck by

the opportunity furnished in the bays of the Debating room for wall decorations of a kind entirely new, at least in England.   He proposed that the walls should be covered with a series of tempera pictures illustrative of scenes from the " Morte d'Arthur," a work which had at this time a special attraction for him, and from which he took the subjects of many water-colour paintings.   His idea was acceptable.   The funds of the Union would not, however, allow the committee to give a commission to the painters.

Chiefly through the agency of Mr. Bowen, now Sir Charles Bowen, Lord Justice of Appeal, who was the President of the Union, and was very helpful to the scheme, an arrangement was made by which all incidental expenses, material, scaffolding, travelling charges, &c., should be defrayed by the club, the artists contributing gratuitously the remainder of the work.

Rossetti entered with characteristic enthusiasm into a scheme which was calculated at every point to appeal to him, and during the year 1857 he busied himself continuously in interesting other artists in the project, and in obtaining their co-operation.   Thus, beating up for recruits, he obtained the co-operation of Mr. J. Hungerford Pollen, who near that time was Proctor at the University, Mr. E. Burne Jones, Mr. William Morris, Mr. Val Prinsep, Mr. Arthur Hughes, and Mr. Spencer Stanhope.   Some difficulty was experienced in securing the co-operation of Mr. Morris, but this was at length obtained, and in the close of 1857 the work began.

A month was the time assigned by Rossetti's sanguine mind to the execution of the task.   Successive causes of delay surged up, however, and six months were spent before it was accomplished, and the tempera designs, which are popularly, but inaccurately, from the technical point of view, spoken of as frescoes, were finished.

The result, so far as the present generation is concerned, is failure, and the pictures have peeled away until, at the present moment, they are not decipherable. The walls were new, and were not properly prepared—not, indeed, having even been flattened. These compositions, accordingly, which, at least, attracted in their time some attention, are lost. Rossetti was responsible for Sir Lancelot before the Shrine of Sangreal, a work which was never quite finished, the purposed completion being abandoned, when it was discovered that the whole was doomed to perish. A design of Rossetti's presenting Arthur seated with his Knights at the Round Table, was carved in stone and coloured by Mr. Munro, and now appears in the tympanum of the porch.

In itself this abortive scheme has no special interest. By the intimacies into which he was thrust, however, a strong influence was brought to bear upon Rossetti personally, and art and literature are likely to look back to these Oxford days as marking an epoch. With those associated with him in the execution of the task Rossetti was previously acquainted. His intimacy with Mr. E. Burne Jones had begun in London a few months previously, and his influence appears to have been strong enough to have induced his new friend to take up the profession of painting, in place of entering the church, as had at one time been intended. While Rossetti and Mr Burne Jones were at work on the paintings, Mr. Swin burne entered the room, and introduced himself to both artists. The friendships then contracted were no less permanent than those previously made. Rossetti's friendly and affectionate feeling to Mr. Burne Jones, Mr. Morris, and Mr. Swinburne, taking these names in the order in which the acquaintance was made, lasted to the end of his life. He lost sight of Mr. Swinburne, however, towards 1872, and Mr. Morris towards 1877. Mr. Burne Jones he saw so late as the Christmas before the final departure for Birchington.

CHAPTER IX.

AFTER the death of his wife, Rossetti found the
chambers he occupied with her too charged with
painful memories to be tolerable. He went for a short
period to stay with his friend, Mr. Madox Brown, at Highgate Rise ; then, after a brief residence in Lincoln's Inn
Fields, he took a lease of the house at No. 16, Cheyne
Walk, possession of which he retained until his death.
Though unprovided with a studio that fully answered his
requirements, this fine old building, with its handsome iron
gates, its frontage commanding the river, and its extensive
garden, formed an almost ideal residence for him. The
conditions under which it was taken had, however, no
element of possible permanency. Joint occupants with
Rossetti were Mr. Swinburne, Mr. George Meredith, and
Mr. William Rossetti. That four men of individualities
so potent, and, in some senses, so aggressive, or at least
assertive, as those of the men named, should be able to
live together in closeness of continuous intimacy, from
which there was scarcely an escape, was barely conceivable. Mr. George Meredith, accordingly, made no long
stay. Next after him Mr. Swinburne departed. The
two brothers held on, as was natural, for some time

longer, the younger, in this, as in every other case, assist-
ing the elder with counsel, not always followed, and
in the early days with money. This association, which
never involved continuous residence on the part of Mr.
William Rossetti, ceased upon his marriage in 1874,
after which date Rossetti occupied alone this house
which had always a chamber vacant for a friend. His
entry upon this new habitation took place, assumably,
about October, 1862. On the 23rd of this month he
writes: "I suppose I shall sleep in Chelsea to-morrow."
On the 7th of January of the following year a letter is
dated from Cheyne Walk. Since the destruction of
the rooms in Chatham Terrace, Cheyne Walk is alone
associated, so far as London is concerned, with his
memory. Whatever other residence he occupied after
this time was in the country. His relatives and most
intimate friends recall him at the Manor House, Kelmscott, near Lechlade, a house which, near 1869, he
occupied jointly with Mr. William Morris. More than
one long stay was made at Penkill Castle, in Ayrshire,
where he and Mr. W. Bell Scott were guests of Miss Boyd.
Mr. Theodore Watts and Mr. George Hake were with him
for a time at Bognor. More than one visit was made
to the houses of friends, his disappearances in later
years being due to failing health. With Cheyne Walk,
however, most recollections of Rossetti are associated.
The house he crowded with quaintly-carved oak furniture,
and other beautiful and costly objects in which he delighted. Here his fine collection of blue china was
exposed to view, or was employed, regardless of risk, at
the dinner parties, which he was fond of giving. Here,

too, were gathered, not all at the same time, the motley collection of animals, peacocks, armadilloes, the wombat, woodchuck, or Canadian marmot, and other outlandish creatures, including the famous zebu, which last animal is the subject of the only surviving story presenting Rossetti in a light absolutely comical. That Rossetti was greatly struck with the beauty of this animal, and that he induced his brother to join him in purchasing it for £20, is certain. Large as was the garden at the rear of 16, Cheyne Walk, in which the beast was to feed, no access to it was possible except through the house, the passages in which were tortuous, and of no great width. A veritable bull in a china shop, then, the zebu had, with the greatest care, to be carried, firmly bound and lassooed, into its destined home. Here, for a time, it remained fastened to a tree, and was duly exhibited to visitors. Rossetti, meanwhile, at a safe distance, dwelt upon its beauties, and pointed them out with his maul stick. According to the testimony of Mr. Whistler, whose well-known waggishness casts, perhaps, a faint shadow of suspicion on the story, the fierce little animal, which was not much bigger than a Shetland pony, nursed a sullen resentment against the indignities to which he was subjected. One day, when the two were alone in the garden, and Rossetti was contemplating once more the admired possession, and pointing out with the objectionable stick the points of special beauty, resentment blazed into indignation. By a super-bovine exertion the zebu tore up by the roots the tree to which it was attached, and chased its tormentor round the garden, which was extensive enough to admit of an exciting chase round the trees. Finally Rossetti was enabled to escape from his pursuer, whose freedom of movement had, fortunately, been hampered by the disrooted tree. The animal had now to be got rid of, at any cost, and, as a purchaser was not to be found, it had to be given away. With renewed precautions, it had to be carried back through the house. No smash occurred in either progress, and the zebu finally went its way. That the story is true in all its details, or that imagination has done nothing to supply colour, may be doubted. Rossetti, in subsequent years, when discussing his pets, past and present, was not much given to talk of the zebu.

Here, lastly, were held those meetings, prolonged often until the early hours of the morning, which to those privileged to be present were veritable nights and feasts of gods. Here in the dimly-lighted studio, around the blazing fire, used to assemble the men of distinction or promise in literature and art whom the magnetism of Rossetti's individuality collected around him. Here Rossetti himself used, though rarely, to read aloud, with his voice of indescribable power and clearness, and with a bell-like utterance that still dwells in the mind, passages from the poems he admired ; and here, more frequently, some young poet, encouraged by his sympathy, which to all earnest effort in art was overflowing and inexhaustible, would recite his latest sonnet. So far as regards years, this is anticipating a little. While on this subject it may, however, be said that Rossetti's appearance at this period, especially when, during later years, to his own annoyance, he had got a little fat, has often been compared to that of Shakespeare. Mr. Gosse says it reminds him rather of

Chaucer. Making allowance for difference of size, since
Rossetti was not more, probably, than five feet seven
inches in height, and for training, as regards deportment
and voice, Rossetti, in physical appearance and in speech,
may be said to recall Signor Salvini. In complexion and
some other respects the resemblance was striking, and
there was, in addition to similarity in the shape of the
head, about both in private life the same appearance of
placid strength.

About 1865–6, Rossetti, who was at that period strongly
disposed to social pleasures, joined the Arundel Club,
an association of painters, journalists, actors, and others
which met, and still meets, in Salisbury Street, Strand.
He was for many years a member of the Garrick Club.
In the Arundel, however, at which the meetings were less
formal, and which then numbered among its members
Mr. F. Sandys, Mr. J. M. Whistler, Mr. Albert Moore,
Mr. George Chapman, Mr. Thomas Jeckyll, Mr. Anderson
Rose, and other friends of Rossetti, he sought to unbend
himself. The experiment, so far as he was concerned,
was but moderately successful. An attempt to join the
whist players resulted in fiasco. For whist Rossetti had
an absolute disqualification, and no amount of respect or
attachment to his genius could reconcile players to a
partner who ignored or scorned the elementary rules of
the game, and who could only be regarded as a third
enemy.

In connection with his membership of the Arundel
Club, however, an event hitherto unrecorded took place.
This was an exhibition of pictures by members of the
club, to which Rossetti sent several important works. No

catalogue of this exhibition is preserved, and an unassisted memory may not attempt to say what the works were. The exhibition, however, was a conspicuous success, and inspired much interest. Rossetti also exhibited some paintings at the Hogarth Club. Nor were these the only exhibitions to which he sent paintings or drawings. Altogether inadequate were, it is needless to say, these exhibitions to do more than stimulate curiosity concerning Rossetti's powers. It was reserved for the Royal Academy to substitute for the appetising tastes of Rossetti's work, which had previously been afforded, a full and satisfying drink. Concerning the fitness of this proceeding some doubt may be expressed. That the Academy, which in the lifetime of Rossetti had accorded him no slightest courtesy, should upon his death pose as his patron, and should itself reap the profits of the tender interest which the premature death of the brilliant poet and painter was calculated to inspire, seems scarcely fair to the family by which Rossetti had been constantly and conscientiously aided, and to which he would himself have bequeathed whatever profit his name, as a part of his possessions, was worth.

The first portion of Rossetti's residence in Cheyne Walk was fairly happy. He was never tired of admiring the trees in the garden, one tree, a sycomore, especially, which may be traced in many of his pictures, and he found much pleasure in the quaint animate nature with which he was surrounded. He began at this time to write with something like regularity to his mother, whom he always addresses in terms of the utmost affection. To her he describes, August 16, 1864, how "the peahen has hatched two out of her four eggs, and now stalks

about with two little whining queernesses at her heels, no
bigger than ordinary chicks, but perhaps a little steadier
on their pins;" and tells her, which may cast a light upon
his conscientiousness in labour, that he has spent a week
in getting roses for his picture, and has had honeysuckle
sent him from all parts of England. To Mr. Madox Brown
he utters complaints which he keeps from his mother
about the difficulty in the way of finding purchasers for
his best work, the constant cry of painters, in his case
fully justified. The only thing to do is, he says, to stick
to water colours, in order to live. "It is disgusting," he
says, in August, 1864, "to do such ' sloshy' work at all "
("sloshy" was with him a favourite word of contempt);
"but as soon as I do better the dun is at the door, so
needs must."

In November, 1864, he took a fresh trip to Paris,
stopping at the Hôtel de Dunkerque, 32, Rue Laffitte.
On this visit he was taken by "Fantin" (Fantin-Latour,
the painter of L'Hommage à Delacroix) to see Édouard
Manet, the pupil of Couture, who the year previously had
startled Paris by his marvellous picture of Le Déjeuner sur
l'Herbe, in which nudities and modern costumes were
strangely blended. He speaks also of Gustave Courbet,
the founder of the realist school, whose labours in France
had gone in some respects in the same direction as those
of Rossetti in England, and who subsequently presided
over the destruction of the column in the Place Vendôme.
With the works of these men Rossetti was but moderately
impressed. Courbet's paintings, he holds, have great
merits in parts, but "are all most faulty." He speaks of
"this incredible new French School—people painted

with eyes in one socket, through merely being too lazy
to efface."

The results of the death, a year or two earlier, of Mr.
Thomas Edward Plint, of Leeds, an early collector of the
young school of English painters, carried dismay into
many studios, and among others into that of Rossetti.
Commissions had been liberally distributed by Mr.
Plint, and very considerable sums had been paid on
account of pictures not yet finished. The affairs of Mr.
Plint upon his death were not wholly satisfactory, and
the sale of his pictures and the realization of his assets
became necessary. Among the pictures in Mr. Plint's
collection were Mr. Madox Brown's great picture Work,
one of the masterpieces of the so-called Pre-Raphaelite
school, and very many paintings by Rossetti, Millais,
Hughes, Wallis, and others. The collection was exhibited in London, and was sold by auction. The result
of the sale in 1865 was anything rather than encouraging
to painters of the younger school. Rossetti speaks of
things being desperate, and states in one of his letters
that works of his colleagues which were purchased at
£250 each were sold for £30 and £60, and condoles
with his correspondent that " your being bought in at
£550 and my £84 were the triumphs of the sale." One
more thing in connection with painting which he mentions
in his correspondence is that he has just had lent him his
old first picture, The Girlhood of Mary Virgin. Of this he
says, " I can look at it a long way off now as the work of
quite another ' critter.' " It is satisfactory to learn that
he finds it a long way better than he thought.

One or two purchases which he makes near that date

inspire him with enthusiasm. In one case he writes : " I have just bought for £2 a most god-like picture of the Old Swan Inn and Market Place at Barnet." This he calls a *chef d'œuvre* of the British School, and thinks is by Morland in his best time. " But really," addressing his correspondent, he continues, " it would ravish your innermost soul, only it has got holes knocked in it, and so I must get it in hand at once." The second purchase which took place when he was staying at Tenterden, in Kent, assumably two years later, *i.e.*, in 1866, is of a different kind. It consists of a box-tree cut in the shape of an arm chair. He saw it at the door of a cottage where it had been trained by the inmates since 1833. The old woman to whom it belonged sold it to him for a sovereign, and he sent it to Chelsea where it was at once to be planted. He tells this to his mother, to whom he confides his intention of sending the vendor, who moves his compassion, a second sovereign upon its arrival. With Winchelsea, whither he proceeds, he is much struck, forwarding to his mother an account of the procession to inaugurate the session. This, he continues, " may give you some idea of the doziness of the place, which is more to my taste than any other I know. Every one is 82 if he is not 96."

About 1867 Rossetti made a strenuous, but not too successful, effort after earlier hours. To Mr. Madox Brown he complains pathetically, " I have no chance of seeing you now, for a new doctor has told me to be in bed by twelve, and I'm trying to do it." The doctor in question, whose advice coincided with that of others of his profession previously consulted, appears to have been

Sir William Jenner.   Jointly with Mr. Sandys he under-
took about this time what he considers a "friendly duty"
towards Mr. Swinburne, whose "Poems and Ballads" had
drawn upon him many discomforts.   To his brother he
defends this interference, though he adds that "the
genius displayed in his (Mr. Swinburne's) works" is not
benefited "by association with certain accessory tendencies."   In a letter to his mother, whom he addresses
constantly as "Dear good Antique," or by a score of names
caressingly frivolous, he writes under date May 12,
1868, *àpropos* to his fortieth birthday : "The reminder of
the solemn fact that I am a man of forty could hardly
come agreeably from any one but yourself.   But considering that the chief blessing of my forty good and bad
years, has been that not one of these has taken you from
me, it is the best of all things to have the same dear love
and good wishes still coming to me to-day from your dear
hand at a distance, as they would have done from your
dear mouth had we seen each other."

In this year, 1868, the first trace appears in his letters
of the insomnia, which, aggravated by so-styled remedies,
was to be the curse of his life.   Penkill Castle, Ayrshire,
was re-visited in September.   On his way Rossetti spent
a couple of hours in the Exhibition at Leeds, finding time
to notice "a most glorious Sandro Botticelli" (a Nativity),
"a very fine Carpaccio," and "splendid heads by Titian,
Moroni, Bellini, and Velasquez."   Upon his arrival at
his destination he is delighted with the place, adding, "I
slept better last night than I have done for a long time."
After this declaration, sufficiently ominous when read by
the light of his later life, he mentions having consulted

Bader, the oculist of Guy's Hospital, with regard to his eyes, from which he suffered much, and detects in his mother's "dear letter a *funny* old intention of writing large for the benefit of my sight." "This," he adds, "would be quite in the antique spirit." Upon his return he sends his mother his sonnets, which he describes as a "band of bogies," and fancies them joining with the skeletons of various closets to entertain her by a ballet. With humour characteristically quaint in its blending of extravagance and mysticism, he continues : "Their shanks are rather ghastly, it is true, but they will keep their shrouds down tolerably close, and creak enough themselves to render a piano unnecessary. As their own vacated graves serve them to dance on, there is no danger of their disturbing the lodgers beneath, and, if any one overhead objects, you may say that it amuses them perhaps, and will be soon over, and that as their hats were probably not buried with them, these will not be sent round at the close of the performance."

An extract from a letter addressed to a male correspondent is thoroughly characteristic of his feelings with regard to those he thought in any serious way interested in art, and of his prejudice against those belonging to academic circles. "I am very much grieved to hear of poor Payne's death. He was a good fellow, a good friend, and a man of true inclinations to good things in art and poetry. It is singular how these rare birds, whether patrons or critics, get picked off one by one, while no man ever heard of the putrid academic sty being a pig the worse for all the epidemics and cattle plagues that turn up."

CHAPTER X.

TOWARDS the close of the year 1869 Rossetti was busily occupied with preparations for his forth-coming volume of poems. To his mother he speaks, August 21, 1869, of printing some old and new poems, chiefly old, which he promises to show her in proof. The reason advanced is, "I thought it necessary to finish them as I found blundered transcripts of some of my old things are flying about, and would at some time have got into print perhaps, a thing afflictive to one's bogy (spirit)." With his brother William, to whom the task of revision is entrusted, he discusses the omissions that he will make. "I believe," he says, "I am likely to cut out 'Mary in Summer,' 'The Choice' (three sonnets), and the 'Bullfinch Sonnet.' I hesitated to print 'Ave' be-cause of the subject, but I thought it well done, and so included it. Sonnet, 'French Liberation of Italy,' I have removed from the second section, and shall not replace." In the directions concerning the revision of proof he asks his brother to be careful as to the punctuation, a matter which he always regarded as important. "In punctua-tion," he writes, "I have my own ideas, which may not be yours, so I will ask you generally to leave this alone."

The changes prospective or actual which he makes are too numerous to be dealt with. A few, however, are of interest to those who study his manner of work. To "Sister Helen" he affixes a first stanza, on the recommendation of Mr. William Bell Scott, who held that without this the impression of what was going on was not perfectly distinct. This criticism of Mr. Scott is just. Something may, however, be urged in favour of the bold commencement originally planned, the dramatic fitness as well as the abruptness of which is very fine. He debates the propriety, in "Stratton Water," after the lines—

> " The kine were in the byre that day,
> The nags were in the stall "—

of re-writing some stanzas which had dropped out descriptive of the gradual impression on Lord Sandys of his recognition of the girl whom he thought dead, and seeks counsel whether it would be better to re-insert them. Apparently the answer to this was in the affirmative, since the two descriptive stanzas which now follow the lines are not necessary to the action, are not in the general ballad style, and are apparently introduced for the purpose of explanation. Of "My Sister's Sleep," which, as has been said, is one of the earliest poems, he declares that it is very distasteful to him, and that he would not insert it were he not afraid of surreptitious copies getting into print. A poem called "Song and Music" he omits.

At this period the exhumation of the MSS. had not been made, and the poems dealt with were those which had been recalled by memory, existed in collections, or were in the possession of friends. The exhumation in question took place apparently on the 6th or 7th of October, 1869. On the 13th of the same month he mentions to his brother that the manuscripts are in his possession. Friends, he states, had hinted from time to time at the possibility of the buried poems being recovered, and when he had been in Scotland the previous year, Mr. William Bell Scott had recurred to the subject. What appears to have brought the matter to a head was the offer of a friend, Mr. Charles Augustus Howell, of his own accord to take charge of the execution of the task. Rossetti was still averse from the proceeding. Eventually, however, he yielded a reluctant consent, and "the thing was done." An order had of course to be obtained from the Home Secretary, who proved to be an old and rather intimate friend of Rossetti, Mr. H. A. Bruce. All was found as it was left, but the book, though not in any way destroyed, was soaked through and through, and had to undergo a long process of ablution in the hand of the medical man who assisted Mr. Howell. By his care also the whole was dried leaf by leaf. There seems reason to fear, Rossetti writes, that "some minor portion is obliterated, but I must hope this may not prove to be the most important part. I shall not, I believe, be able to see it for at least a week." To his brother he apologizes for not telling him earlier, saying, "It was a service I could not ask you to perform for me, nor do I know any one except Howell who could well have been entrusted with such a trying task." It was necessary to employ a solicitor in the proceedings, since some difficulties were raised by the cemetery authorities, naturally anxious to be assured that nothing of the nature of a fraud was involved in the disinterment of the MSS. Three days later, after seeing the book, which "will take some days yet to dry," he declares it is in a disappointing, but not hopeless state. The only further reference to the poems previous to publication which calls for notice in his letters is the information supplied to his brother : "You know I always meant to dedicate the book to you. This I shall of course do." As all readers of the volume, which now, apart from its other merits, is a bibliographical rarity, are aware, the volume is dedicated to Mr. W. M. Rossetti.

"Poems by Dante Gabriel Rossetti," as the first volume is called, was published on terms eminently advantageous to Rossetti by his friend, Mr. F. S. Ellis, then of King Street, Covent Garden, and subsequently of Bond Street. By the lover of Rossetti's poems it will always be valued on account of containing the first version of many of the poems, and one sonnet which has been omitted from the collected "House of Life," and from the general collection of works. Seventy-four sonnets, eleven songs, and twenty-six longer poems were selected by him as worthy of preservation. Of the contents "The Blessed Damozel," "The Staff and the Scrip," and "My Sister's Sleep," have already been discussed. Of the remaining poems "Sister Helen" is the most important.

In this the romantic and the dramatic aspects of Rossetti's genius attain their highest development. The poem in its class is less unequalled than unique. In his employment of a burden to a ballad, if not in the ballad generally, Rossetti is happier than Mr. Morris, happier even it may be than Mr. Swinburne, to name the poets who were led by influences of association, and kindred studies, to practise similar forms of composition. With the general work of Mr. Swinburne, who is unequalled in lyrical fervour, and has enriched English verse with a greater variety of metres than any other poet—it may almost be said than all other poets—to compare that of Rossetti would be preposterous. In some domains, however, and notably in the sonnet and the ballad, Rossetti may stand by his side. The ballad especially commended itself to Rossetti's imagination and his taste. His admiration of it dates from the time when he read with avidity the earlier ballad literature of England and Scotland. There is, however, little affinity between his work in this direction and the masterpieces by which he was stimulated.

"Sister Helen " is, in fact, a dialogue with a slightly varying chorus, spoken, it may be assumed, so far on the principle of the Greek chorus that its utterance depicts the feelings of some, in this case imaginary and unseen, spectator. As a tale of calm and inexorable vengeance on the part of a wronged woman, it is unapproached in literature. Medea herself is neither more fateful nor more relentless than is Sister Helen. In the stanzas which Rossetti added in his later years, and included in the issue of 1881, the nature of the offence perpetrated by the victim of Sister Helen's conjurations is stated. Owing fealty to her, he has taken to his bed another bride. Three days have elapsed since the wreath has been placed upon the bride's head, the three days during which the groom's body has melted away into death, even as the waxen image has melted before the fire. The stanzas in which this information is conveyed are in all respects equal to the remainder of the poem, and the variations of the burden are so striking and so character-istic of Rossetti that, once given, their removal would be intolerable. The last letter ever written by Rossetti, dated April 5, 1882—he died on April 9th—was to the writer of these lines, and communicated the news that he had ventured on an addition to the poem, a proceeding which he knew was likely to be regarded by his correspondent with no great favour. This letter will be given in its proper place. It is pardonable to maintain that the effect of the added revelation diminishes the spectral terror of the poem, a fine element in which is its appalling vagueness and mystery.

The superstition on which "Sister Helen" is based, though old assumably as antique times, has in years quite recent, difficult of credit as this may seem, been known to be practised. Among the pretensions of witchcraft ex-posed by Reginald Scot in his "Discovery of Witchcraft," the first edition of which appeared in 1584, is "A charme teaching how to hurt whom you list with images of wax, &c.," with directions how to frame in virgin wax the image of the individual to be killed, and with what magical additions or unguents to bedeck or smear it. The customary treatment was to stick pins in the image, the result of which was supposed to be the death of the individual simulated. A second method was to melt the waxen image before the fire, the consequence being that as the wax dissolved the person it was sought to injure would melt and die in torments. This is the plan adopted by Sister Helen. The process is watched by the brother of the woman who has resolution enough to carry it out. His inquiries as to the meaning of what is taking place, and his comments upon the action outside the house, supply the action of the poem. A couple of stanzas will show the treatment.

> " ' Why did you melt your waxen man,
>   Sister Helen?
> To-day is the third since you began.'
> ' The time was long but the time ran,
>   Little Brother.'
>   (*O mother, Mary Mother,*
>   *Three days to-day, between Hell and Heaven!*)
>   *   *   *   *   *
> ' Oh the waxen knave was plump to-day,
>   Sister Helen;
> How like dead folk he has dropped away.'
> ' Nay now, of the dead what can you say,
>   Little Brother?'
>   (*O mother, Mary Mother,*
>   *What of the dead, between Hell and Heaven?*) "

From the balcony into which he ascends the child sees the objects that go by. Three riders in turn appear to supplicate pity for the man who is being slain. Two are the brothers of the dying man, the third the " mighty Baron " Keith of Keith, his father. Their petitions are delivered by the child, and are received with grim, cynical, and fateful comment by Sister Helen, who watches the figure disappear until the bell from over the hill tolls the dying knell of her victim, the wax figure drops, and the flames win up apace. Her crime accomplished, the penalty has instantly to be met. This is indicated in the last verse—

> " ' Ah ! what white thing at the door has cross'd,
>   Sister Helen ?
> Ah ! what is this that sighs in the frost ? '
> ' A soul that's lost as mine is lost,
>   Little Brother ! '
> (*O mother, Mary Mother,*
> *Lost, lost, all lost between Hell and Heaven !*) "

" Sister Helen " is a poem to which no extracts can do justice. It must be read as a whole. Each verse is practically inseparable from the other, and the slow accumulation of scarcely defined horror is part of the mystery and might of the poem. Slight as are the changes of the burden, they are weighty in significance, and the answers of the heroine, with their grave acquiescence in the soul's death, which she knows is the price of her deeds, have dramatic force that is indescribable. Some suggestion of the name of his characters may have been found by Rossetti in the marvellously fine poem of Sydney Dobell, one stanza of which is—

> " She makes her immemorial moan,
>   She feeds the shadowy kine.
> Oh Keith of Ravelstone,
>   The sorrows of thy line ! "

In every other respect the poem is original in inception and execution, nor can this adoption of a fairly familiar name be held in the slightest degree to impair its originality.　In sombre mystic beauty and passion, in the use of the supernatural, and in that most eminent of poetic gifts, the extorting from inanimate things an enforced sympathy with, and response to, human aspiration and suffering, or even, as it almost seems, a stake in human destiny, " Sister Helen " stands alone among contemporary work.　We have to go back to the powerful and unblessed imagination of Webster to find anything equally bold, original, and tremendous.

To the same class of composition belong two other poems in the first collection, " Troy Town " and " Eden Bower."　Both are much later works than " Sister Helen," having been composed shortly before the publication of the volume, and with a view to their appearance in it.　There seems something incongruous in assigning to a story such as " Helen of Troy " what may perhaps be called a Gothic setting.　Justification can be found in the writing of previous poets who have adapted classical legends to the music of their day, or that of their choice.　Rossetti, however, was little given to draw precedents from the works of others.　It is interesting, accordingly, to be told by Mr. Hall Caine that, in his later years, Rossetti thought less of this poem than he did upon its appearance.　The construction is happy, the central line ringing its changes upon the phases of "the heart's desire."　The latter portion of the burden—

> " O Troy's down,
> Tall Troy's on fire "—

is neither very musical nor very significant.　Neither

Venus nor her suppliant has any very distinct individuality. Perhaps the finest part in it is that in which the
effect of Cupid's shaft is seen, and Paris

> " Turned upon his bed, and said,
> Dead at heart with the heart's desire,
> ' O, to clasp her golden head.' "

In his best workmanship, however, Rossetti guards against
the recurrence of such sounds as " bed," " said," and
" dead," which occur practically within half a line.

In "Eden Bower" what was most mystical in Rossetti's
mind was called into play, and was applied to a difficult
subject. That the legend of Lilith, according to Rab-
binical mythology, the first wife of Adam, a species of
witch, whom Goethe introduces into " Faust," and who,
in spectral shape, is still held to haunt the air, appealed
strongly to him, is shown by the fact that he painted
Lady Lilith once in oil, and often in water-colour or other
medium. A powerful study of snake-like seduction, and
witchery, and of burning and implacable hatred is afforded.
The picture of Lilith in the opening stanza—

> " Not a drop of her blood was human,
> But she was made like a soft, sweet woman "—

explains at once the weirdness of the conception and its
want of human sympathy. The period during which a
subject such as this had attraction for Rossetti was not
long, and it is fortunate for his fame that it was not.
Monstrous embraces and passion semi-animal, semi-

diabolic are not easily rendered conceivable or attractive. For one person who reads "Eden Bower" and "Troy Town," a score study the "House of Life," or dwell upon "A Last Confession," and "Jenny."

CHAPTER XI.

"A LAST CONFESSION" is the most dramatic poem Rossetti has written. Without resembling any individual work of Mr. Browning, it seems due to the inspiration of that writer. So essentially original is Rossetti, a trace of imitation, conscious or unconscious, is scarcely to be found. Keen admiration and close study of a man's work beget, however, a species of rivalry, and "A Last Confession" appears to have been written under some such influence. Like many of the poems recently described, it is a story of vengeance. The passion, however, that is displayed is human and masculine, and there is no element of *diablerie* such as burns lurid in Sister Helen, and creates in Lilith a shuddering revolt. The Italian character of the hero, and of the background of the story, renders the avowal of murder on the part of the hero conceivable. A man, for his loyalty to his country a wanderer and an outcast, has learnt to love the girl whom he has adopted. To the priest, when dying, he tells the story of her adoption, of his growing love, of her responsive affection, the change to coldness that comes over her, the fear of her future degradation, and the sudden assassination.

Fragmentarily and inconsecutively the events are narrated by one whose dying hours are haunted by the vision of his victim, now fair and tender and trusting, now unwinding from her side the thick dark hair, wet with her blood, and smiling on him as she essays to draw from her side the dagger he has planted there.   Psychological study, keener than Rossetti often affects, marks the progress of the narrative, and the shuddering avoidance by the narrator of all mention of the murder, even when the point is reached at which a description of the event seems imperative, is admirable.   Consummate art is shown, moreover, in the recurrent waves of interruption, and in the species of attempted vindication, when the final spur to action is said to have been the recognition of the resemblance between the laugh of the murdered girl and that of the "brown-shouldered harlot," to whose coarse, empty mirth he had listened in the fair.   Lovely touches are afforded when he describes the sudden pity that smote him when he thought that the child, appealing to him, had been left by her parents to God's chance—

> "Because of the great famine, rather than
>   To watch her growing thin between their knees.
>   With that, *God took my mother's voice and spoke*,
>   And sights and sounds came back, and things long since,
>   *And all my childhood found me on the hills.*"

It is perhaps natural that the soul of the painter should speak through the mouth of his hero.   The portrait of the heroine is, unlikely to have been given by one, whatever his opportunities of seeing early art, who had not

undergone Rossetti's training in the worship of special
forms of beauty. There is at least more of Rossetti
than of any hunted Italian patriot in the description of

> " a mouth
> Made to bring death to life—the under lip
> Sucked in, as if it strove to kiss itself.
> Her face was ever pale, as when one stoops
> Over wan water ; and the dark crisped hair
> And the hair's shadow made it paler still:—
> Deep-serried locks, the dimness of the cloud,
> Where the moon's gaze is set in eddying gloom.
> Her body bore her neck as the tree's stem
> Bears the top branch ; and as the branch sustains
> The flower of the year's pride, her high neck bore
> That face, made wonderful with night and day.
> *   *   *   *
> Her great eyes,
> That sometimes turned half dizzily beneath
> The passionate lids, as faint, when she would speak,
> Had also in them hidden springs of mirth,
> Which, under the dark lashes evermore
> Shook to her laugh, as when a bird flies low
> Between the water and the willow-leaves,
> And the shade quivers till he wins the light."

The language of passion is often poetical. In this
case the illustrations and the perceptions are scarcely
noticeable as those of any man except Rossetti himself, or
an associate in the P.R.B. In one passage, indeed, of
this poem the mystical turn of Rossetti, in his earliest
poems, asserts itself. This is the description of the
dream of the garden of God, which visited the murderer
on the eve of the confession. The women walking in
the garden are, as he says, known to him from their

painted images in the church. The account, however,
how "the sun flared a spent taper," and the picture of
the blessed maidens who

> " Threw their tresses back,
> And smote their palms, and all laughed up at once,
> For the strong, heavenly joy they had in them
> To hear God bless the world"—

are conceived in the very spirit of "The Blessed Damozel."

With "A Last Confession" it is natural, if only for
the sake of contrast, to associate "Jenny." The first
draft of the later poem belongs probably to a period
so early at least as 1853, when Rossetti began the picture
of Found, the resemblance of which to it in subject has
naturally been pointed out. Its form, as it at present
exists, was assigned it at a much later date. Together
with certain of the sonnets belonging to the " House of
Life," " Jenny " has aroused some opposition. It has,
however, found many strenuous defenders. The subject,
especially the personal aspects of the relationship
pourtrayed, is calculated to wound certain suscepti-
bilities and violate the precepts of English society, which,
whether to its praise or blame, has always been more
squeamish concerning names than things. It is futile
to point out that in France the reticences of this poem
would be regarded as more remarkable than its avowals.
Between the literatures of France and England there is
a gap not yet at least to be bridged. In defence of
"Jenny," it is to be urged that there is no violation of
sanctity, as well as no picture of evil. All that can be
brought against it is that it presents, with some few, slight

touches of realism, scenes that occur nightly whenever civilized or half-civilized masses are drawn together, that it stops short of any form of passion or vicious proceeding, and that it furnishes material for a series of reflections upon the conditions of modern society, and is filled with a manly pity for feminine weakness. The defence of the subject it is needless to undertake. The poem itself is perhaps the most essentially human in the volume. The banter, which in its course the author chides himself for directing against the heroine, is, in fact, directed against human nature, and the poet accepts a full share in the amount of condemnation involved. So.long as the world and humanity remain what they are, men will indulge in speculations such as Rossetti herein puts forth. The execution meanwhile is equal to the level of Rossetti's best work, and has a species of humour and tenderness more familiar in his spoken words, and in his correspondence, than in his printed writings. A book written for universal perusal is different from a poem which appeals to the cultivated alone. When then the theme of a poem has to be indicated rather than shown, it is difficult to quote a passage even. Here are, however, a few lines which have the spirit of Hood, with a grace and refinement beyond the reach of Hood, true poet though he was—

> " For sometimes, were the truth confess'd,
> You're thankful for a little rest,—
> Glad from the crush to rest within,
> From the heart sickness and the din,
> Where Envy's voice at Virtue's pitch
> Mocks you because your gown is rich,

> And from the pale girl's dumb rebuke,
> Whose ill-clad grace and toil-worn look
> Proclaim the strength that keeps her weak."

One phrase illustrative of the moral of the poem, which is conveyed in Othello's memorable words, " O, the pity of it ! " is quite Divine.   It is that in which, likening Jenny to a rose shut in a book, he says—

> " Yet still it keeps such faded show
> Of when 'twas gathered long ago,
> That the crushed petals' lovely grain,
> The sweetness of the sanguine stain,
> Seen of a woman's eyes, must make
> Her pitiful heart, so prone to ache,
> *Love roses better for its sake.*"

" Stratton Water " is a ballad thoroughly different in type from those previously mentioned.   It has no burden, and is, in fact, a direct imitation of the style of the old ballads of the borders, some of the naïve humour of which, as well as the style of treatment, is caught. Unlike almost any other long poem of Rossetti's, it has a happy termination—

> " Now make the white bed warm and soft,
> And greet the merry morn ;
> The night the mother should have died,
> The young son shall be born."

Some importance is attached to " Dante at Verona," since Rossetti selected it to give a title to his promised volume, and as the earliest in date of the important poems, it heads the Collected Edition of Rossetti's works.   It is moreover a species of complement to his translations from the Italian, and an essential portion of the tribute of reverence and affection which the family paid to the great poet of mediævalism. The touching story of Dante's exile, and of the shelter afforded him at the Court of Can Grande della Scala, is sympathetically told, and the poem, though somewhat of the nature of a scholastic exercise, is sustainedly elevated in thought and diction. It is a little formal, however, and in too heroic a strain, as when it presents the attitude of Dante to the Jester in his host's house as that of loathing.

With "The Burden of Nineveh" it is helpful, in a sense, to compare the fine poem of Mr. Bell Scott, "The Sphinx, considered as the Symbol of Religious Mystery," which probably belongs to a period not widely different. Both poems contrast, as is natural, the present time with that of which the object addressed—in Mr. Scott's case, "The Sphinx;" in Rossetti's, a winged bull from Nineveh in the British Museum—is representative. "Across the centuries" Mr. Scott hears "the clang of Coptic hammers" round "the limbs half freed," or watches, in later years the Cenobite, as he "hurries half naked by" striking the idol "with his crutch and palsied hand." Before this sublime antiquity the interests of the present seem but fool's play, and the modern generation shrinks

> " Into small grasshoppers or clamouring storks,
>   That build frail nests on roofs of kingless towns."

Not wholly dissimilar is the strain in "The Burden of Nineveh." From the time when, within the shadow of

the great winged bull, Sennacherib knelt, and Semiramis
brought, in offering, incense and zones of gold, to that
last year, when to another God the Christian knelt and
prayed, Rossetti passes.   His reflections, have, however,
a quaint, half-serious humour, characteristic of Rossetti,
who pictures the files of school children learning to view
the idol " as a fact, connected with a zealous tract," and
anticipates some future day in which possibly the beast
may be borne away by some coming race, "a relic of
London—not of Nineveh," and may even, by its presence,
give rise to doubt as to whether Londoners walked in
"Christ's lowly ways," or bowed "unto the god of
Nineveh."   A rather fantastic notion is perhaps this, but
such commended themselves to Rossetti.   The other
miscellaneous poems belonging to this first volume may,
with the exception of " The Stream's Secret," be dis-
missed.   In " The Stream's Secret " Rossetti is once
more at his best.   That worship of collective womanhood which informs his poetry is here, as in other cases,
focussed in an imaginary individual, to his love for whom
he strives to make Nature respond. It is pleasant to learn,
on the authority of Mr. Sharp, that the stream from
which the poet strives to wrest the secret of love is the
Penwhapple in Ayrshire, which runs through the grounds
of Penkill Castle, the residence of his friend, Miss A.
Boyd.   To the same authority we owe the knowledge
that the poem was written in 1869.   " The Stream's
Secret " is elaborated with signal care ; its music has
something of the waters' flow, and its cadences are more
caressing and dream-like than those of any other poem
of Rossetti—it might almost be said of any poem of the

epoch. In the first stanza the recurrence of words is
eminently poetical and suggestive :

> " What thing unto mine ear
> Wouldst thou convey,—what secret thing,
> O wandering water, ever whispering ?
> Surely thy speech shall be of her.
> Thou water, O thou whispering wanderer,
> What message dost thou bring ? "

The employment of alliteration is also singularly judi-
cious. It has not the antithetical happiness of Mr.
Swinburne's " Lisp of leaves and ripple of rain," or of
Milton's "Most musical, most melancholy," but it is the
more effective from being at first scarcely observed. The
notion that the verse is alliterative scarcely presents itself.
Inspection shows, however, that no less than ten words
in the stanza begin with *w*. How successfully the rhymes
are used is at once apparent, the whole possessing a slow
broken harmony, the effect of which is inexpressibly
lulling. The same gifts are noticeable throughout the
entire poem, which, while it possesses no such glowing
hues as some of its predecessors, has ineffable delicacy
of colour as of form. In this poem, as in certain of the
sonnets, Rossetti paints with a warmth of colour that
incurred some subsequent censure. In the following
exquisite picture even there is a frankness of revelation
that is not common in poetry :

> " Beneath her sheltering hair,
> In the warm silence near her breast,
> Our kisses and our sobs shall sink to rest ;
> As in some still trance made aware
> That day and night have wrought to fulness there,
> And Love has built our nest."

So delicate and fragrant is the whole that we should no
more think of censuring it than of condemning the
divinely hardy passages in " Cymbeline," containing perhaps the highest tribute to purity ever written, in which
Iachimo stealing into the room in which Imogen is
sleeping, declares, in what sounds like a lover's rapture—

> " 'Tis her breathing that
> Perfumes the chamber there."

and notes—

> " On her left breast
> A mole, cinque-spotted, like the crimson drops
> I' the bottom of a cowslip."

From first to last " The Stream's Secret " is a gem.

At this period, so far as regards his poetry at least,
Rossetti seemed almost to have broken away from the
religious ecstasy that colours his early work, and even
to have quitted for a while the mysticism that exercised
a more abiding influence. For perfection of workmanship the Laureate might be proud to claim this poem,
which for the rest breathes a spirit not altogether unlike
his own.

As a translator Rossetti has had few equals. An
effective translation from a poet can only be accomplished by an equal. Rossetti was more than the equal
of Villon, the inspired poet of the bordel and the gallows,
and his translation of the famous " Ballade des Dames
de temps jadis" is a marvellous instance of conquest over
difficulties. It is perhaps impossible to find in English
any absolute equivalent to the burden of the ballad " Ou
sont les neiges d'antan ? " But " Where are the snows

of yester-year ? " is a very bold and poetic attempt to grapple with the difficulty. Villon's " Lay ou Rondeau sur la Mort," and the " Ballade de Villon à la requeste de sa Mère pour prier Notre-Dame" are no less well rendered. " John of Tours," which is described as old French, is especially touching, and " My Father's Clerc," from a chanson which used to be sung by Mrs. Burne Jones, is supremely delicate and graceful. One or two translations from the Italian, in one case from Rossetti himself, are included in the second volume, and two others executed about the beginning of Rossetti's poetic effort—say 1847-8—appeared in *The Athenæum.*

There remain the sonnets. In writing these Rossetti took extreme pleasure, and his success was in proportion to his zeal. His graver thoughts seemed to flow naturally into sonnet form, as his lighter ideas concerning persons and things took the shape of nonsense verses, of which he composed an indefinite number, many of them ex- tremely whimsical. Upon the sonnet meanwhile he lavished the wealth of his imagination and the treasures of his research. Whatever words most noble, graceful, picturesque, or significant he could, by thought and research, add to his vocabulary were reserved for his sonnets. These he polished and recast with the same earnestness that he devoted to his pictures, and his youthful work was not seldom entirely re-shapen. The principle on which he wrote was that in each sonnet a thought should be crystalized and wrought into a gem. In his workmanship he does not rigidly adhere to one form of construction, though most of his best sonnets accept what must be considered the regular form, the opening

octave with its rhymes doubled, and the closing sestett with
them alternate. By this rule he was not, however, closely
bound, and many sonnets may be advanced in which the
two last lines of the sestett consist of a rhymed couplet.
Reserving until the volume of 1881 is considered "The
House of Life," which therein first saw the light in its
complete form, it is easy from the remaining sonnets to
gain an idea of Rossetti's method and aim. In one
respect the sonnet to the memory of his father, entitled
"Dantis Tenebræ," comes short of the ideal Rossetti
subsequently framed. The portion of the thought con-
stituting the octave is not completed within that limit,
but overlaps the sestett. It may almost be said, moreover, that the language here is less elaborate, and the music
less fervent than in other sonnets of the same period.
For such shortcoming, explicable enough in itself, if
shortcoming it be, there is full compensation in the
mystical significance with which it is charged, and in the
biographical revelation it affords.

> " And didst thou know indeed, when at the font,
>   Together with my name thou gav'st me his,
>   That also on thy son must Beatrice
> Decline her eyes according to her wont,
> Accepting me to be of those that haunt
>   The vale of magical dark mysteries
>   Where to the hills her poet's foot·track lies,
> And wisdom's living fountain to his chaunt
> Trembles in music? This is that steep land
>   Where he that holds his journey stands at gaze
>   Tow'rd sunset, when the clouds like a new height
> Seem piled to climb. These things I understand ;
>   For here, where day still soothes my lifted face,
>   On thy bowed head, my father, fell the night."

In his sonnets, as in his pictures, Rossetti is indeed of those that " haunt the vale of magical dark mysteries." Not seldom the words he chooses are ennobled by the use to which he forces them ; the observation of Nature that is supplied is of her remote suggestion and latent significance ; and things are charged with an amount of symbolism, the full influence of which the poetic nature alone can grasp. So deeply impressed with the symbolism of most things in Nature was indeed Rossetti, that he incurred, as is known, the charge of coarse realism. To his mind sanctities were inherent in human relations, and the notion of finding uncleanness in homage, even though physical, was scarcely to be conceived.

As is the case with most imaginative natures, Rossetti's mind was filled with a vague unrest. What, in letters and poems, he chose to call indolence in himself, was frequently aspiration after unattainable closeness of relation with beauty. At the end of his sonnet on "Autumn Idleness" this species of yearning is fully illustrated—

> " While I still lead my shadow o'er the grass,
>   Nor know, for longing, that which I should do."

The joy that Wordsworth felt in Nature does not come near Rossetti. Like Jaques he "chews the cud of sweet and bitter fancy," but the fancy is more frequently bitter. The trees whisper to him " what he feared to know." In the case where he is moved by music, it only

> " In regenerate rapture turns my face
>   Upon the devious coverts of dismay."

His fancy even, a gift which, though rarely exercised, he possessed in an eminent degree, is more often grotesque and, so to speak, boding, than happy. Once in the sonnets of the first volume, he has a conception equally graceful and quaint when he sees the deer "dappled white and dun" grazing from "hillock eaves," and holds it is

> " As if, being foresters of old, the sun
> Had marked them with the shade of forest leaves."

His most reckless indulgence in fancy is in the remarkable sonnet "A Match with the Moon," in which, walking merrily, he dogs "the flying moon with similes," and finds her now "like a wisp" in ponds, now "caught in tree-tops like a kite," and anon "in a globe of film all vapourish," swimming "full-face like a silly silver fish," until, when the road turns and she gets behind him, she sends his "wizened shadow craning round" at him. In spite of the pleasant farewell when she kisses him for good-night, the whole effect is weird, elfish, and uncanny. "On Refusal of Aid between Nations" is striking in the political lesson it reads. Anything rather than a politician was Rossetti, whose views upon things political and theological, though influenced by those of his brother, of Mr. Ford Madox Brown, and other associates, were less advanced than theirs. In the separation of interests, the incapacity to combine to resist oppression or wrong, and the indifference of the non-stricken to the sufferings of the stricken he felt—

> " We know
> That the earth falls asunder, being old."

This view was strongly held. Here lies its chief interest.
Its importance or significance relating to other influences
need not be discussed.

The majority of the sonnets in the volume of 1870 not
belonging to the " House of Life " are for pictures, of
which ten are for works of his own. These can with
difficulty be fully comprehended except by the light of
the pictures themselves. The most human of these is
that of Mary Magdalene at the door of Simon the
Pharisee, in which, however, the zeal, warmth, mysticism,
and personality of the Roman Catholicism to which
Rossetti, while remote from it in conviction, was close in
sympathy and imagination, are strongly illustrated. This
is especially the case in the closing lines. In the drawing,
Mary, seeking to break from a festal procession and enter
a house in which is Christ, is held back by her lover.
The last six lines are—

> " Oh, loose me ! See'st thou not my Bridegroom's face
> That draws me to Him ? For His feet my kiss,
> My hair, my tears, He craves to-day ; —and oh !
> What words can tell what other day and place
> Shall see me clasp those blood-stained feet of His ?
> He needs me, calls me, loves me ; let me go."

The contrast between the monosyllabic intensity of this
and the sustained amplitude of treatment, and magnifi-
cence of phrase ordinarily used, is very striking. In the
above lines there are only two words, both compound, one
wholly Saxon, " Bridegroom " and a second Saxon in
part, " blood-stained," that attain to more than one
syllable. A lesson on Rossetti's workmanship is afforded

by a comparison of this sonnet with that on Pandora, in which, dealing in no very classical spirit with a classical subject, he employs such phrases as the " Olympian Consistory " and " Powers of the impassioned hours prohibited."

CHAPTER XII.

DURING the years over which the composition of the poems included in the first collection extended, Rossetti's reputation as a painter had been established. On his progress in art it is superfluous to dwell. So linked and interwoven are, however, the two forms of accomplishment in Rossetti that they are mutually helpful and explanatory. Not easy is it to divorce one from the other. Apart from the direct influence of such long developed study as that of Dante, the picture as was natural continually begot the poem and the poem the picture. With the choice of two media, in the use of both of which he was equally proficient, Rossetti made naturally frequent experiments as to which was the better adapted to his powers. To this moment the question remains unanswered. Unlike some poets, however, who have employed verse for the purpose of illustrating problems, polemical and metaphysical, with the result that they are regarded as poets among philosophers and as philosophers among poets, Rossetti has been received with enthusiasm in both capacities by both poets and painters. It may, indeed, be said that he is a painter's painter, and a poet's poet.

Difficult as was, through deficiency of early training, the task of draughtsmanship, he could, when the occasion vindicated or exacted the effort, draw with surprising accuracy and vigour. As a colourist his reputation is unsurpassed, and the warmth and splendour of his workmanship have won general recognition. More important, however, than any technical skill was the imaginative and creative power displayed in his paintings, the smallest and obscurest of which, if such terms can be applied to one who gave forth no work that was not carefully planned, are informed with soul, while the greatest soar beyond reach of easy comparison.

Through his entire career his Dante worship asserts itself. In those famous water-colours with which, for the most part, his life was occupied between his gradual estrangement from what was narrowest in Pre-Raphaelitism and the establishment of his reputation,—productions which constitute in some respects his most interesting works,—one of the earliest was Giotto painting Dante's Portrait—a thoughtful, beautiful, and admirably finished design. Earlier even than this, in 1849 and 1850, he had drawn in pen and ink the triptych, Il Saluto di Beatrice, the execution of subjects from which subsequently occupied him. In 1852 he painted in water-colours the design for the left division with the motto " Guardarmi ben ; ben son, ben son Beatrice." This subject shows the meeting in Eden of Dante with Beatrice, who, with veil backwards drawn, gazes sustainedly at the poet. A replica of this design was executed in 1864. To an early period belongs the execution of a design from the " Vita Nuova," representing Dante surprised by visitors on the anniversary of the death of Beatrice, and Beatrice denying Dante her salutation. Francesca da Rimini is ascribed to 1854. Shortly afterwards was painted in water-colours Dante's Dream at the time of the Death of Beatrice, also taken from the "Vita Nuova," reproduced in oil in 1870; and noteworthy in the reproduction, as the largest work which the conditions of art and art-patronage allowed Rossetti to paint. This picture, which some have held Rossetti's masterpiece, and of which Sir Noel Paton, quoted by Mr. Sharp, says: "Fifty years hence it will be named among the half-dozen supreme pictures of the world," was purchased in 1881 for 1500 guineas by the Corporation of Liverpool, and is now in the Walker Art Gallery in that city. Beata Beatrix is a study in crayons, from the "Vita Nuova," of which the result was a lovely oil painting of the same name, subsequently (1863) executed and purchased for the collection of Lord Mount Temple. This is another of the painter's most masterly efforts. A list indeed of the paintings illustrative of Dante and his influence would under such conditions as now exist become a mere nomenclature. It is needless, accordingly, to do more than mention the famous triptych of Paolo and Francesca, the centre of which represents Dante, conducted by Virgil through hell, passing the lovers ; while the right compartment shows the famous kiss after which they " read no more that day," and the left their penance, the Madonna Pia, and the portraits of Dante. Of the subjects of poems in the first volume which Rossetti treated pictorially, Lilith, is that which for a short period he most affected. This witch wife of Adam appealed to Rossetti's imagination by her magical associations no

less than her physical loveliness. Between the commencement of the fine oil painting of the beautiful,
sensual, and fateful face, and its completion, Rossetti
gave to the world no less than five separate works, so
entitled, on which, as indicative of the character of its
beauty, he bestowed the name Lady Lilith. Pandora,
Sibylla Palmifera, The Passover in the Holy Family, and
Venus Verticordia, are also fine pictures to which illustrative poems are supplied.

Among the works of importance between which and
the poems no direct connection can be traced, though in
these even it is continually possible to see the influences to
which the poems owe their genesis, a few stand prominently forward. Foremost among these is the triptych for
Llandaff Cathedral. The various divisions of this are
curious as exemplifying the boldness with which at this
period and subsequently Rossetti threw off the trammels
of Pre-Raphaelitism, and while adhering to the mysticism,
the recurrent phases of which mark his entire life, hesitated not to employ costume and effects which commended
themselves by picturesqueness and beauty rather than by
archaical correctness. In richness of colouring and in
impressiveness this work remains one of the most striking
oil paintings of Rossetti's middle period. The water-
colours include many subjects from the " Morte d' Arthur,"
the influence of which is more perceptible in Rossetti's
painting than in his poems, not a few supplied by a per-
sistent study of Mr. Browning, and miscellaneous works
covering the whole of classic and romantic literature, with
some the subject of which is modern. In these what is
characteristic of Rossetti is seen at its best. Until a few

years ago the mention of such works as Bocca Baciata,
Fair Rosamond, Lucrezia Borgia, The Blue Bower, The
Beloved, and a score of other works, finished in execution,
and displaying the most fervent imagination, would have
conveyed little to any except a privileged circle. Now,
however, the value and significance of these pictures, of
the crayon and pencil drawings, and of the book illustrations are generally known and enthusiastically acknow-
ledged. That pictures, for which in the period of struggle
the painter could not obtain the modest sum barely
sufficient to fill his mouth and supply materials for further
efforts, should be subsequently bought for more pounds
than the painter asked shillings, by the State or by private
purchasers, is in no sense an individual grievance. Hard-
ships and penury are at the outset the usual attendants of
an artistic career and constitute probably in the main a
stimulating and beneficial experience. Rossetti's grievance was that during the best and most productive period
of his life, which unfortunately was not the latest, he was
unable to paint his subjects in the dimensions which
their importance demanded, and that works had to be
compressed within small canvases which for their due
development required greatly increased space. There
are few lovers of art, who, looking at such small and
exquisite works as many of those named, including a
whole series of Dante pictures, and again of pictures such
as the Hamlet and Ophelia, do not experience regret
that national encouragement of art seems impossible, and
that our collections are enriched, not by works which the
artist could paint for fame, but by those which he has
executed while " cabined, cribbed, confined " by circum-

stances over which he has no control.   Comparatively
few words of complaint are to be found in the correspondence of Rossetti, whose Italian blood failed to find the
relief in grumbling which northern natures experience;
but the necessity of painting what he can sell, rather than
what he wishes, is a source of constant heartache.   In
his later years Rossetti obtained great prices for his
pictures.   It is certain that the success of the volume
of 1870, by bringing him prominently before the public,
raised the monetary value of his paintings.   Taking,
however, into account the quality of his paintings, and
the amount of conscientious labour he put into them,
the prices obtained in his palmiest days were far from
extravagant.   For such works indeed of subsequent years
as the Bella Mano, the Astarte Syriaca, and the Veronica
Veronese it is difficult to conceive what price future days
will regard as excessive.

Of Rossetti's painting as a whole, into the details of
which it is impossible to enter, it may be said that its
qualities are those in which English art is, as a rule, most
deficient.   Apart from the mastery of colour which is conceded to Rossetti by those to whom the types of beauty
he affected appeal least directly, the qualities inherent
in his pictures, as in his poems, are dramatic force and
passion, mysticism, and symbolism, which differ from
those of early art in being voluptuous rather than ascetic.
Rossetti's reverence takes the nature of adoration.
There would have been little cause for surprise had he in
his early years fallen in with that retrograde movement
to ancient forms of faith which came as an attendant
upon a renaissance in art.   This, however, he escaped,

and although to the end of his life he had reverence for the mysteries of Christianity which, on many sides, appealed to him, and even showed a sort of half disposition to turn to its teachings for comfort, he remained unattached to any set of theological views. In his work generally, however, he was a worshipper; and much of transcendentalism and devotion characterizes his pictures of womanhood. To the full extent he obeyed the maxim " *Quod Deus puricavit tu commune ne dixeris.*" Beauty was with him the object of pursuit, and the mystery of its significance is such that all effort after its attainment, and all homage rendered it, were in his eyes essentially reverential. It is by this light that his work, poetical and pictorial has to be studied, and some of the difficulties which have been felt with regard to portions of the "House of Life," and to such subjects as Lilith, will disappear. A few pictures of later date may find mention here, and so dispose of this portion of his work.

In oil Water Willow is interesting as a picture of the houses at Kelmscott where Rossetti, with his friend Mr. Morris passed some of his happiest days. Mariana, executed in the same medium, can scarcely be regarded as a study from Shakespeare, but is at least named after the Mariana of Shakespeare. It is a miracle of colour. Rossetti was at times tired of naming pictures. In a fit of petulance he once declares, " I cannot be bothered to stick names on things now; a head is a head." That was, however, but a passing mood. As a rule, if no association inspired the painting of a head, such came during the progress of the work, which was shaped to it. Veronica Veronese and La Ghirlandata, two works in oil, for Mr. Graham and Mr. Leyland respectively, belong to about the same epoch, and are fine specimens of his powers. These were followed by The Roman Widow or Dis Manibus, Fleurs de Marie, and Proserpina, a subject of which Rossetti never wearied. The last-named picture is associated with two sonnets—one in English, and a second in Italian. Meanwhile the list of water-colour paintings, crayon drawings, pen-and-ink sketches, bears witness as much to Rossetti's industry as to his genius. Many of these which are inaccessible to the general public, are visible in photographs. There are few of Rossetti's friends whose private stores are not enriched by these reproductions, unsatisfactory, it need scarcely be said, of some of his manifold works. Through these, even, the beauty and poetry of conception and design, which are scarcely less marvellous than the glory of the colouring, may at least be traced.

The period which immediately followed the appearance of the first volume, and its general acceptance by the critical organs and by the public, was perhaps the most serene, if not the happiest of Rossetti's life. A new future, down the vistas of which he delighted to gaze, opened out before him, and dreams of new work in the same line at once shaped themselves in his brain. Mr. Ellis, his publisher, a close personal friend, had published the book on such terms as young authors seldom obtain. With pardonable enthusiasm, accordingly, he writes to Mr. Madox Brown, " Ellis tells me that he has sold out my first thousand, all but two hundred, and is going to press again at once, and so the two editions at one quarter value of a twelve-shilling book, will bring me three hundred pounds in a few weeks. Not so bad for poetry, after all, even if the public find themselves glutted with the second thousand." To Mr. James Anderson Rose, a close and constant friend, he writes, under the date May 19, 1870, concerning his book: "Its success has surprised me. A second thousand called for in less than ten days! Poetry is likely to prove no such bad trade in England before long." Referring to the long ballad poem he contemplates, about a magic mirror which is a crystal ball, soon to take shape and appear as the noble poem known as "Rose Mary," he says, "I wish one could live by writing poetry, I think I'd see painting d—d." It is possible that a few months later when the storm burst, his views as to the relative pleasantness of the two forms of art might have been found to be changed.

Meanwhile, among the old friends whose faith in Rossetti's poetry had been firm and fervent, there was of course great rejoicing. New admirers, whom the magic of intimacy with a man such as Rossetti converted at once into friends, came around him, and he found himself the centre of a circle of worshippers, including many of those who have subsequently given direction to modern thought. No dissonant note was heard in a chorus of enthusiasm which rose around him. Widely divergent estimates were of course formed of the value of this latest contribution to poetry, but censure was at least respectful in tone, and the writer seemed to be

" Advanc'd above pale envy's threatening reach."

At once like thunder from a clear sky, to use a hack-
neyed figure, came an attack before which the enchanted
fabric of complacency fell to the ground.   In *The Contemporary Review* for October, 1871, appeared an
article signed Thomas Maitland, and headed " The
Fleshly School of Poetry."   Into the origin of this
curiously unprovoked and unjustifiable attack it is futile
to inquire.   Some of the minor minstrels with whom
Rossetti had been more or less closely associated, re-
sented the kind of recognition awarded the volume of
" Poems," all unlike that accorded their own works.   In
the " fierce light " with which Rossetti's poems were
surrounded, the flickering recognition they had themselves received could scarcely be seen.   With hinted
disapproval of the choice of subjects accordingly, they
began to disparage the work, and hold aloof from the
writer.

No motive of past friendship, however, reduced to feeble
muttering the censure of Mr. Thomas Maitland, a critic
who, speaking in terms of solemn arraignment, publicly
likened Rossetti to authors of whom it may be said, as Sir
Thomas Browne said of " sins heteroclitical," that there is
" a sin even in their histories," and that of them there
should remain no " register but that of hell."   It was with
amazement that Rossetti heard that the indignant Scot,
who " came from a remote retreat in the Highlands to
this great centre of life which men have named London,"
with a mission to rebuke vice and to expose iniquity by
linking the writings of Rossetti with the foulest outcome
of depravity and disease, was himself a poet long resident
in London.   " What do you think ? " he asks his brother,

under the date October 17, 1871, "—— writes me that Maitland is Buchanan." There is little temptation to drag back to the light of day particulars, now buried, of a feud which, though in some future edition of "The Quarrels of Authors" it may move the mirth of our descendants, will always leave an ill-taste in the mouth of those who have the highest interests of literature at heart. For his imputations Mr. Buchanan had the grace ultimately to apologize. That the original offence was heightened by the publication in pamphlet form with his own signature, and with justificatory additions of the article, cannot perhaps be held. Rossetti himself wrote at some length in protest against his assailant, and "The Stealthy School of Criticism"—an unwise step which gave rise to much subsequent controversy. His friends, moreover, came to his aid, and replied in terms of no measured indignation, contempt, and wrath. Smarting under imputations of motive and lash of censure, Mr. Buchanan, after the authorship was fixed upon him, was in no mood for penitence. During some years accordingly the attitude of hostility was maintained, and it was not until the pother was over that sane reflection induced Mr. Buchanan to dedicate a work to the subject of his quondam assault, and in so doing to withdraw his arraignment. One quotation alone from a letter of Rossetti addressed to the writer of this sketch shall be given. It is to this effect. " You may be sure that these monstrous libels—both the pamphlet and its press results—cause me great pain, but I have been in doubt what course to take till this evening, when it seems clear to me that I have the right to adopt a tone raising me above the question.

I have no part in insult or violence, and cannot be involved because their atmosphere is raised around me." This letter, unfortunately dated only " Monday night," is thoroughly characteristic, and the resolution to have no part in insult and violence, belongs to Rossetti's innermost nature.   In a letter from Mr. Buchanan, forming a portion of his amends, which is given as a note in Mr. Hall Caine's "Recollections of Rossetti," the writer speaks of his pamphlet being "a mere drop of gall in an ocean of *eau sucrée*."   That it could have had on Rossetti the effect Mr. Hall Caine has described, he can scarcely believe, and he adds, "Indeed, I think that no living man had so little to complain of as Rossetti on the score of criticism."   Not very logical is all this, though it is perhaps natural. The fact that a man has known nothing but praise does not prepare him to receive censure with equanimity.   A succession of hot baths is not the best preparation for a plunge into iced water, or even for the receipt of a discharge of mud.   Rossetti had obtained full recognition.   His nature was robust as well as tender, and a hostile criticism would no doubt have startled him, and perhaps have acted as a healthy stimulus.   There is, however, a difference between literary criticism and moral indictment. Weak spots may easily be found in the literary armour of Rossetti, from whom some important gifts are wanting.   That a man, however, who had won in art and letters the praise and sympathy of all whose approval was worth having, whose bosom friends and associates in youth had risen to the topmost place in their professions, and who throughout his career had found all that was earnest in art clinging to him with devotion, and appealing to him for counsel, should see himself held up to infamy as a deliberate assailant of virtue and corrupter of his age, was enough to shock and to pain. Shocked and pained Rossetti accordingly was, and his early demise is due indirectly to the disturbance thus caused. In those long nights of insomnia which grew increasingly frequent, he dwelt upon the cruelty and the outrage to which he held he had been subject, and the resort to chloral hydrate grew correspondingly easier and more constant.

Exteriorly his life was peaceful and calm. At no time were the gatherings at Cheyne Walk more interesting or more brilliant than they were in 1871 and the first half of the following year, and never did the host, when he substituted the *rôle* of speaker for that of listener, grow more eloquent or more convincing. To a circle drawn round the fire in the studio, while the greater portion of the room remained in twilight, Rossetti would read with his unequalled voice and delivery some passage from a favourite author, and would make this an excuse to draw from some young and but half-reluctant poet his latest sonnet. The interest Rossetti took in these compositions did not cease with the words of encouragement he was ready to utter. If the poem commended itself to him, and any flaw in its perfection seemed capable of removal, letter after letter with suggestions for alteration would come to the writer at his house. So many as half-a-dozen separate letters have been written by him on consecutive days for the purpose of dealing with a crux in a sonnet. How rare is friendliness such as this, and how rarer is the sacrifice of personal vanity, must be at once obvious.

No less evident is it how calculated was such interest to light in the minds of those around him, the kind of devotion which attended Rossetti in life, and is still consecrated to his memory. The room, meanwhile, had other guests besides its human occupants, and the tenant of a sofa was likely enough to be startled by the appearance from under a pillow of a wood-chuck, a wombat, or some other animal equally outside the range of ordinary sympathies.

CHAPTER XIII.

AFTER the pleasant enthusiasm begotten of the success of his volume and the memory of his feud grew more distant, Rossetti, partly for the purpose of carrying out his conception of poems, partly on account of ill-health and insomnia, was more frequently, and for longer periods, absent from London. His migrations are traceable in his correspondence with his mother and other members of his family. In conjunction with Mr. William Morris, he took The Manor House, Kelmscott, Lechlade, in Gloucestershire, on the Upper Thames. Apart from their personal interest, his letters from this and other haunts are valuable, as showing the schemes he formed of new work before he found respite from suffering in collecting the materials for his second volume. The idea of writing a play on the subject of Pompey appears to have commended itself to him. He expresses surprise that Shakespeare, who "seems to have given more perfecting labour to Roman subjects than to any," should have left this alone, and adds, "I suppose the most faultless by far of his plays is 'Julius Cæsar.'" Another scheme which commended itself to him was the translation of the poems of Michael Angelo. Under the

date of January 10, 1873, he writes to his brother, " I am
writing to Ellis for the most recent exhaustive edition of
Michael Angelo's poems, &c. (if so there be). I mean to
translate and edit him at odd times." Five days later he
recurs to the subject, and says, " My own impression is
that Michael Angelo stands almost alone as a good Italian
poet after Dante, &c., unless we except Poliziano."
Schemes for pictures accompany those for poems. One
from the life of Michael Angelo strongly commends
itself to him, but appears not to have been begun.
" Condiva tells us," he says, " that he heard Michael
Angelo, when quite old, say that he regretted nothing
more than that when he visited Vittoria Colonna on her
death-bed he did not kiss her face, but only her hand.
This interview would make a noble picture, and I think
I ought to paint it as a companion subject to my Dante's
Dream. I suppose the omnivorous French School have
nobbled it somewhere, but I don't remember to have
seen it done." This story forms the basis of the not very
successful sonnet, " Michael Angelo's Kiss, No. xciv." of
" The House of Life." Of the Proserpine on which he
is then engaged he says it will be his best picture.
Among unrealized schemes is a visit to be made, in
company with his brother William, to Italy, which was
strongly pressed upon him by his friends, and to which
in his letters he frequently recurs. In case of visiting
Vasto he is anxious to avoid any form of public recognition, such as his father's son was sure to receive. The
best thing to be done, he holds, would be " to go to the
very quietest and most Italian places that could be heard
of," an aspiration that speaks of the nervous shrinking

from general intercourse which the use of narcotics was causing, and must not be taken as indicative of his general feeling with regard to Italy.

The first literary work upon which he now engaged was the publication of the second edition of his translations from the Italian Poets. This work furnished him with pleasant occupation. To his mother he says, " I am meaning to dedicate to you the new edition of my Italian Poets. The first was dedicated to poor Lizzy, and I had some thought of retaining the dedication with date, but this seeming perhaps rather forced, I shall substitute your dear name in the second edition."

Poetry, at this time, commended itself strongly to him. Under the influence of his more lately found friends, and especially of Mr. Theodore Watts, whose services to him and to literature are beyond reach of acknowledgment, he had resumed the composition of sonnets. He seems at this time to have made closer observations of Nature, and to have found pleasure in her mysteries and beauties closer than had previously been evidenced. His letters of this period, 1873, contain passages of delightful description. Of a poem he sent to *The Athenæum* he says, " It is one I wrote when first I came here (Kelmscott), and embodies a habit of the starlings, which quite amounts to a local phenomenon, and is most beautiful and interesting daily, for months together, in summer and autumn." This poem appears in the second volume under the title of " Sunset Wings." His descriptions are ordinarily those of a painter : " The river growths have continued to develop one after the other. The arrow-head rush puts forth eventually a most lovely staff of blossom just like a little sceptre. The way that the white blossom grows triple round the staff is most lovely, and the whole might really be copied exactly in gold for a sceptre. . . . The white lily in the garden has grown to a perfect decorative cluster." Some of his descriptions of the animals around him are humorous. A comically fat and stolid Iceland pony, that was only on two occasions seen to do anything but eat in his private field, and on these occasions leaned against a tree to meditate, moves his mirth. His favourite subject is, however, a dog of the name of "Dizzy," belonging to his companion and secretary, Mr. George Hake, which like himself displays an untoward propensity to growing fat. On one occasion an attempt was made in the dog's interest to reduce him on a diet of dog biscuits. He became gradually more and more dejected, until one morning he ate a stone instead, which, reappearing on the hearth-rug, convinced his master that he must not be reduced to despair.

The death of his old friend James Hannay brings out a fine aspect of Rossetti's character which it is impossible to ignore, but which none the less, after his death even, there is some delicacy in approaching. A subscription for the family, which had been left with no very brilliant position, was begun, and to this Rossetti gladly contributed. To Mr. Ford Madox Brown he writes to the effect that he has no superfluous means, but he supposes that it will not do him so much harm as it will do the recipients good, and adds that he very much prefers subscribing, say £10, to the printed list, and giving the rest privately to the family, so that he may not " swell it

in the circular." The subscription is sent through his
brother, to whom he expresses his great desire to do
more, adding, " Of course, any help I could render would
be limited enough, but, at any rate, I have no family of
my own to provide for, and am therefore doubly bound
to do what I can for an old friend's children."

One more letter to his mother from Kelmscott, where
some gleams of happiness still broke upon him, places
the relationship between the pair in a golden light. It
is dated February 23, 1874. "I have often thought
of you since we last met—always whenever my path in
the garden lies by the windows of that summer room at
which I used to see your dear beautiful old face last
summer. . . . To-day the little Morris girls collected
all the flowers we could find in the garden—no very
choice gleaning—and they were sent on to you, so perhaps you have them ere this reaches you. I know they
will be better than nothing to your flower-loving heart."

A couple of years later, January 21, 1876, he pays
her a compliment such as a mother seldom receives from
a son of equal distinction. " What you say of Haydon
shows how clear and lucid your mind is at an advanced
age, and how well and incisively you can express your
conclusions. I assure you that your first inculcations on
many points are still the standard of criticism with me,
and that I am often conscious of being influenced
correctly by these early-imbibed and still valuable
impressions."

A passage from a letter to a friend shows Rossetti in
his most riotous mood of description : " —— got here
at last, after which he whirled us for three days in a

tornado of lies, and was off again, probably on his way
to the Walpurgis nacht.   Three a.m. gave place to 5 a.m.,
as bedtime before the house was clear of him, and
reputations fell thicker than the trees in the last great
gale."

Towards the end of 1876 his correspondence alters in
tone, the writer being more and more depressed.   From
Broadlands, Romsey, the seat of Mr. Cowper-Temple
(afterwards Lord Mount-Temple), he writes to his mother:
"I must tell you that my bodily state is very suffering, and
that my nights are something of which it would be difficult
to convey to you an idea for utter unrest and frequent
severe pain."   During his residence he supposes that at
least fifty or sixty visitors have " stayed and gone " without his seeing one of them.   Of his hostess he says, " You
would simply adore her Christ-like character."

Near this period he resumed his life at Cheyne Walk.
The old social conditions were, however, not realized.
Apart from other pernicious effects, chloral hydrate had
separated him from most of his friends, and converted
into a comparative recluse one of the most sociable of
men.   A few chosen companions rallied around him,
and friends, at the head of whom stood Mr. Theodore
Watts, the closest of his associates, and most fervent
and valuable of allies, yielded him the constant com-
panionship which at this time became indispensable.
During nearly four years Rossetti scarcely, if ever,
quitted his own residence, such exercise as he took being
confined to the garden at the back of the house.   Such
conditions were the worst conceivable for a man whose
illness had taken the outward shape of hypochondria,

and whom nothing, not even the negotiations for the sale of his great picture, Dante's Dream, to the Corporation of Liverpool, nor the preparation of his new volume of poems, could rouse to continuous activity or permanent interest in life. From Herne Bay, where he made, in 1877, a long stay, he writes to his mother declaring that "absolute want of occupation is rotting my life away hour by hour." To his sister Christina he also writes, his letters, though brief, being very affectionate and very sad in the revelations of change they afford.

In 1881 the second volume of poems made its appearance, under the title, "Ballads and Sonnets." In no respect of value or interest does it yield to the earlier volume, and in its possession of the completed series of sonnets, entitled "The House of Life," a portion only of which appeared in 1870, it establishes paramount claims upon attention. "Rose Mary," the opening poem, is regarded by many as its author's highest poetic accomplishment. It is, at least, a magnificent ballad, using, with unrivalled effect, a mystical Eastern conception, and charged with the subtlest and the most poetical significance. Something like the description of the stone itself is the language of the poem—

> " Rainbow-hued through a misty pall,
>   Like the middle light of the waterfall."

The idea is old of a magic crystal in which to the eyes of pure maidenhood the action passing at a distant place stands revealed. Such a conception belongs to the same order of *diablerie* as the waxen image which furnishes the idea of "Sister Helen." Reginald Scot, in "The Discoverie of Witchcraft," refers to the fairy Sibylia, who can be conjured into a crystal stone, and who is likely, unless bound by solemn adjuration, to work mischief. With his marvellous power of quickening with spiritual meaning, and intensifying with passion, the fantastic conceptions which came to his hands, Rossetti has given for tenants to the beryl stone which answers to the crystal sphere, "Fire spirits of dread desire," whose mission it is to lure to their destruction those whom sin has brought within the range of their powers. Mysterious and fateful as any dream of old mythologies are these unseen spirits, of whom we know nothing except through their own half-warning, half-jubilant chaunt; and the limitation of the exercise of their sorcery to those who have "let in defile-ment" in no way diminishes their spectral terror. It would be difficult to make more than Rossetti has made of this subject. Rose Mary attends the coming of her future lord. Her mother, who knows of his approach, and of the perils with which he is menaced by the way, brings once more to her the beryl stone, that the maiden's eyes may, as before they have done, read where and what are the dangers to be shunned. Alas! Rose Mary is no longer qualified to read aright. Her virgin zone has been un-loosened, and the spirits of evil have power over her. By the ruined weir on the river path she sees the glint of spears, and the pennon of her lover's arch enemy, the Warden of Holycleugh, while the upper path is clear from all ob-stacle and danger. Sir James of Heronhaye comes, accord-ingly, by the upper path, and is slain, the love sin between him and Rose Mary being the cause of his death, and of the triumph of the spirits of the beryl. By her misleading vision, Rose Mary's secret has become known to her mother. There is no time for chiding, and none for escaping the calamity. What follows is not directly connected with the legend of the beryl stone. Sorry, indeed, should we be to lose it. Nothing in the first volume of poems of Mr. Morris, with portions of which Rose Mary has much in common, is finer than the description of the appearance of the corpse when it is brought into the chapel—

> " The fight for life found record yet
>   In the clenched lips and the teeth hard set ;
>   The wrath from the bent brow was not gone,
>   And stark in the eyes the hate still shone
>   Of that they last had looked upon.
>
> The blazoned coat was rent on his breast
>   Where the golden field was goodliest ;
>   But the shivered sword, close-gripped, could tell
>   That the blood shed round him where he fell
>   Was not all his in the distant dell."

A new and startling interest is supplied in the discovery by the mother of the dead man's falsehood, and the picture of Rose Mary passing, by the secret path her feet had not trodden before, to the altar, and her destruction of the beryl, would supply a fine subject for a painting, which Rossetti himself might have painted. The poem is, in fact, nobly conceived throughout, and the execution, though unequal, is consonant with the subject. It is better when the poet warms to his work than it is at the outset. Some of the opening stanzas, notably the third,

are weak. The elision necessary to bring the second of
the opening lines can scarcely be made—

> " Daughter, once more I bid you read,
> But now let it be for your own need:"

The compulsion of a rhyme by forcing the accent from
the penultimate to the last syllable, a grace when spar-
ingly employed, as in the lines—

> " The lady upheld the wondrous thing :—
> ' Ill fare ' (she said) ' with a fiend's-fairing,' "

is employed too frequently, and in some cases with an
effect which is fantastic, rather than pleasing—

> " What glints there like a glance that flees?
> Nay, the flags are stirred in the breeze,
> And the water's bright through the dart-rushes."

These inequalities of workmanship constitute, however,
but a small blemish in a work of marvellous power and of
sustained imagination.

"The White Ship" is one of the most dramatic of
Rossetti's ballads. The method of narration of the
calamity, in which the son and daughter of Henry I.,
with three hundred souls, returning from France to
England, perish in mid channel, is happy, the calamity
being described by Berold the Butcher of Rouen, the
sole survivor of the wreck. The use of the burden, not
at the close or in the middle of each stanza, but thrice
only in the poem, is effective. Little in the method

belongs, according to Rossetti's intention, to the early English ballad. The treatment is, indeed, in some respects, French rather than English, but the entire effect is fine, and the description of the death of Fitz-Stephen, when he finds that the prince he sought to save is lost, is thrilling and heroic.

It must add to the grief experienced at the premature death of Rossetti to find that he was capable to the close of writing a ballad such as " The King's Tragedy," with which the list of his productions in this line of poetry closes. That the character of James I. of Scotland, the poet-king whose youth was spent as a prisoner in England, and whose turbulent reign was one long effort to repress the disorders of a kingdom in which violence and crime had reigned unchecked, should appeal to Rossetti, was natural. While taking, however, an historical basis for the story, and adhering so far to the truth as to introduce into his poem some stanzas from James's poem of "The King's Quhair," Rossetti did not hesitate, for the purpose of effect, to depart from strict historical accuracy, especially in regard to the circumstances under which the king, by retiring to the Charterhouse he had erected at Perth, facilitated the operations of his murderers. He naturally retained the supernatural element, which no one who knows his affinities for such subjects will be surprised to find is the most effective portion of the poem, and is, moreover, treated in the very spirit of the old ballads. Less consonant with this ballad spirit is the assigning the task of narration to Kate Barlass, or Catherine Douglas, the heroine of the murder, whose arm thrust through the socket from which the bolt had been withdrawn, is the means of temporarily arresting the assassins.

The historical incidents, the interruption of the siege of Roxbro' hold by the news of the disaffection of the nobles, the rapid return of the king, the arrest of Sir Robert Græme, and the temporary repression of rebellion, are told with spirit. With the start of the regal cavalcade for Perth and the meeting with the crone, whose mysterious predictions fail to turn the king from his purpose, the poem rises into sublimity, and the execution from this point forward is such as Rossetti alone could have afforded. Little in imaginative literature is more noteworthy for weird power and appropriateness than the message of the witch woman—

> " ' O king, thou art come at last;
>   But thy wraith has haunted the Scottish Sea
>   To my sight for four years past.

> ' Four years it is since first I met,
>   'Twixt the Duchray and the Dhu,
> A shape whose feet clung close in a shroud,
>   And that shape for thine I knew.

> ' A year again, and on Inchkeith Isle
>   I saw thee pass in the breeze,
> With the cerecloth risen above thy feet
>   And wound about thy knees.

> ' And yet a year in the Links of Forth,
>   As a wanderer without rest,
> Thou cam'st with both thine arms i' the shroud
>   That clung high up thy breast.

'And in this hour I find thee here,
  And well mine eyes may note
That the winding-sheet hath passed thy breast
  And risen around thy throat.

'And when I meet thee again, O king,
  That of death hast such sore drouth,—
Except thou turn again on this shore,—
The winding sheet shall have moved once more
  And covered thine eyes and mouth."

Supernatural intervention such as this is frequent in ancient poetry and fiction, and is ordinarily futile. Rossetti's employment of it is always prosperous. If ever supernatural interference is justifiable, it is in a case such as this, where through those misty highlands, in which the traditions of wraith and spectre linger longest, a gallant king is riding to his doom at the hands of traitors. In striking contrast with the unpretentious nature of the sibyl is the effect of her presence upon in-animate nature. At the charms of the Lapland witches, "the labouring moon eclipses." Nature, in awe, accords to the spectral presence of the old woman the attention the king refuses, and furnishes the poet with opportunity for those descriptions of the wrath or affright of the earth and heavens, in which he was most at home. The woman, of course, appears once more when the curtain is rising on the tragedy, and equally, of course, her warning voice is once more heard and unheeded, though this time it declares—

" 'Last night at mid-watch, by Aberdour,
  When the moon was dead in the skies,
O king, in a death-light of thine own
  I saw thy shape arise.

' And in full season, as erst I said,
  The doom had gained its growth ;
And the shroud had risen above the neck
  And covered thine eyes and mouth.' "

In the hands of small men supernatural machinery of
this description is a dangerous device ; in those of a
master of the craft its influence is irresistible.   The effect
of this episode, for such, in a way, it is, in binding together the parts of a story the action of which is diffuse,
and in giving the whole tragic dignity and solemnity,
cannot be over-estimated.   Without it the story would be
no more than a fairly spirited narrative ; with it it im-
presses us as do the sombre scenes in a great tragedy.

A few poems, thoughtful, descriptive, and meditative,
and a few sonnets make up, with the ballads mentioned,
and "The House of Life," the contents of Rossetti's
latest volume.   Of these, "Sunset Wings," to which
previous reference has been made, is remarkable with "The
Wood Spurge," as the poems in which Rossetti's observation of Nature in her ordinary phenomena, and apart
from any mystic sympathy and suggestion, is closest.
The opening stanzas might almost have been written
by Wordsworth.   Rossetti, who was no Wordsworthian,
would have been but moderately gratified by a criticism
of this sort.   " The Cloud Confines " has a melody and
fervour almost Swinburnean, and occupies a high position
among Rossetti's latest poems.   Of the miscellaneous
sonnets, several are for pictures.   " Untimely Lost " is a
noble tribute to the memory of Oliver Madox Brown,
whose untimely death Rossetti, in common with all his
friends, deplored.   " Winter" is a peculiarly lovely sonnet,

showing close and observant study of Nature. "Czar Alexander the Second" is interesting as showing that Rossetti, though the son of one who accepted exile for the sake of freedom, was, within certain limitations, on the side of order as against social revolt. Five sonnets to poets Chatterton, Blake, Coleridge, Keats, and Shelley prove who among English poets of the past were, with Shakespeare, the objects of Rossetti's special admiration. The volume bears the following dedication: "To Theodore Watts, the friend whom my verse won for me, these few more pages are affectionately inscribed."

CHAPTER XIV.

B Y a general consensus of opinion "The House of Life " has been pronounced Rossetti's greatest literary work. Strong objection has been taken to the title, which, unless, as has been suggested, the word House is used in the sense attached to it by the astrologers, is indeed in some respects ambitious and misleading. No such justification as warranted Balzac in assigning his own works, the title appalling and presumptuous in any other case, of " La Comédie Humaine," is in this instance to be found. It is necessary, however, to take into account the idiosyncrasy of the man. " The House of Life " is, as has been well said, The House of Love. The part, however, which love plays in life was in Rossetti's opinion so much higher than it is in general estimation, that it is doubtful if the objection had been made to him while living whether he would have attached much importance to it. Rossetti was not slack in regard to his interests. These were, however, a part of the necessities of existence, and no more concerned the soul's life than the discharge of normal functions. For politics he cared little ; of ordinary ambition he had scarcely a trace. Had he been wholly free from some unreasonableness, some weaknesses of vanity and the like, he would have been less human, less approachable, less loveable. His real life was, however, in his affections. His own family he loved with a tender trust that is as rare as attractive to contemplate, and that was, it is pleasant to think, fully returned. Ungrudging service of every kind was rendered him, and not only by his brother, who filled many functions for him between assistant in his work and banker in his need. Those outside his immediate circle, his aunts, the Misses Polidori, and others, were always helpful, as he was glad to acknowledge. The devotion of his friends culminated in that of Mr. Watts, who gave up to him a large share of life. These and other services Rossetti greeted, "Not with vain thanks, but with acceptance boun- teous," repaying in the same kind, and portioning out his life among his friends. When an old friend died, as in an instance before mentioned, Rossetti was willing not only to subscribe to his family to the extent of his means, but to undertake the education of the children at his own charge. The period in which, under the baneful influence of an insidious drug the character and working of which are not even yet understood, he was possessed of idle suspicions of acquaintance once justly valued and guilt- less, in the majority of cases, of the slightest wavering in their attachment to him, may not be taken into account. At this time he was not master of himself, and his vague mistrusts floating like some marsh light from spot to spot, disappearing from one point to appear at another, were the delusions of a disturbed brain. To women he had a kind of loyalty which, if not unknown in other cases, is, at least, reserved to few natures. An attach-

ment, once formed was abiding.   Favour from a woman
involved obligations he was always ready to acknowledge
and meet, and from which no subsequent treachery on
her part would easily absolve him.   Sombre and painful
passages in his life read by this light become intelligible.
By this same light must be studied " The House of
Life," or of Love.   Censure of certain passages in the
portion of " The House of Life " first published influenced
him, and when the completed work was given to the
world one sonnet was omitted in acquiescence with the
judgment of Mr. Theodore Watts, and two or three
passages in other sonnets were modified.   Rossetti was,
however, in these matters silenced rather than convinced,
and the plea in favour of what was misinterpreted remains
in the work itself from which the poems that bred offence
have disappeared.

Before dealing with this defence, it is worth while to
point out that the scheme of " The House of Life " was
modified so far as regards executive details during its
evolution.   In the first volume there appeared, as a portion
of the scheme, various poems, not of sonnet shape, including the passionate " Love Lily," " The Sea Limits,"
perhaps the most divine of Rossetti's short lyrics, " The
Wood Spurge," a short poem of subtlest significance,
"Penumbra," and some others.   These, with some others,
when the second edition was published, appeared under the
general head " Lyrics."   From the " Ballads and Poems "
of the same date they were banished.   The second edition
contained, moreover, none of the sonnets belonging to
" The House of Life " which appeared in the first volume,
their place being occupied with one or two short poems,

and with " The Bride's Prelude," a work of early years
which Rossetti, wisely perhaps, never finished, since in
spite of its quaint mediævalism, its story is purely painful,
and the treatment too stiff and set. The key to the so-
styled indiscretion in "The House of Life" must be
found in Sonnet v. of the completed series. This is
entitled "Heart's Hope "—

> " By what word's power, the key of paths untrod,
>   Shall I the difficult deeps of Love explore,
>   Till parted waves of Song yield up the shore
> Even as that sea which Israel crossed dry shod ?
> For lo ! in some poor rhythmic period,
>   Lady, I fain would tell how evermore
>   Thy soul I know not from thy body, nor
> Thee from myself, neither our love from God.
>
> Yea, in God's name, and Love's and thine, would I
>   Draw from one loving heart such evidence
> As to all hearts all things shall signify ;
>   Tender as dawn's first hill fire, and intense
>   As instantaneous penetrating sense,
> In Spring's birth hour of other Springs gone by."

Love in the individual, according to the rather obscure
utterance of the sestett, or six concluding lines, stands a
portion of the eternal love of the ages past and to come,
a thing in which mortal worship of the best is signified
and sublimated. The reading of the octave is simple.
In the attempt to analyze love, and to separate what
is earthly from what is heavenly, there is in Rossetti's
idea profanity. Soul and body the woman beloved
and responsive becomes a part of the man. The
twain are one, and the love which binds them is the

one Divine effluence not to be distinguished from Divinity. Possessed by this idea, as remote surely from fleshliness as any conception of human relations not wholly passionless, ideal, and futile, Rossetti included in " The House of Life " such sonnets as " Nuptial Sleep," and " Supreme Surrender." The expediency of dealing in any public form with the closest of domestic sanctities is open to question. It is not even justified by descriptive passages of Arcadian love, in which the primitive simplicity of " The Age of Gold " is exposed, supposing these to escape censure. Between the warmest painting of amorous scenes and the revelation, however idealized and symbolical, of the culmination of personal affection, there is a distinct difference. Granting, however, the propriety under any circumstances of such confession, and some of the greatest poets have ventured on it, it is to be expected in a series of poems such as constitute " The House of Life." In the case even of the sonnet subsequently suppressed, the chief objection seems to lie in the use of the word " fawned," as applied to the mouths of the lovers in the last line of the octave. A poet is not to be confronted with philological derivations. It is a part of his privilege, if not of his occupation, to ennoble words by use. In this case, however, Rossetti, while supplying an idea which is physically unattractive, fails to dignify a word of Scandinavian origin which implies almost necessarily something of cringing and servility. The phrase which Rossetti himself employed, in the vindication of his work from the censure passed upon it in " The Fleshly School of Poetry " and elsewhere, is that the sonnet to which special objection was taken embodied, as "its own small constituent share, a beauty of natural universal function, only to be reprobated in art, if dwelt upon (as I have shown that it is not here) to the exclusion of those other highest things of which it is the harmonious concomitant." The "beauty of natural universal function" must be accepted by the light of what is known of Rossetti. A similar plea might otherwise be advanced in defence of the works of aggressive realism with which France has of late deluged civilization. In the case of Rossetti the defence was valid, and is generally accepted.

Taken as a whole, this series of sonnets constitutes in its class the greatest gift that poetry has received since the days of Shakespeare. Individual sonnets as fine as any in "The House of Life" are to be found in Milton, Wordsworth, Mrs. Browning, and other poets. A series such as this, which is, in fact, a life's utterance and a life's story, modern literature does not possess. That passages are obscure, and that the sequence of idea is not always to be traced is true. The same, however, holds good of every poem written under similar conditions and in an approximately similar form. As a whole "The House of Life" is not more difficult of interpretation than "In Memoriam." The opening sonnet, "Love Enthroned," declares that the throne of Love is far above the seat of Truth, Hope, Youth, Fame, and Life, though all these things are in themselves sweet and helpful. That his own art, even with its rewards, was inferior in his eyes to this primal moving heat and worship of love, he admits in assuming that—

"Fame be for Love's sake desirable."

What follows may be summed up in the opening lines of Coleridge's " Love "—

> " All thoughts, all passions, all delights
>   Whatever stirs this mortal frame,
> All are but ministers of Love,
>   And feed his sacred flame."

" Bridal Birth," the second sonnet, illustrates the growth of love by the birth of a child, and with all its sweet spiritual significance is almost as much open to the charge of fleshliness as those singled out for arraignment. It is wholly characteristic of Rossetti, and of no other English poet, to dignify by comparison with the earthly birth the opening life of the soul ; to elevate a " natural universal function," by making it the symbol of spiritual manifestation. How finely, moreover, it is done—

> " Born with her life, creature of poignant thirst,
>   And exquisite hunger, at her heart Love lay
>   Quickening in darkness, till a voice that day
> Cried on him, and the bonds of birth were burst."

Armed and equipped Love springs, and the conquest he achieves is immediate. Succeeding sonnets are full of the adoration, rapturous and playful in turns, which follows surrender when it comes as the fulfilment of a life dream. " The Portrait" (Sonnet x.) is an almost solitary indication of the author's profession. In this, however, the triumph of the painter is not in his skill in his craft ; it is wholly in the thought that— through all time it may be understood—

> " They that would look on her must come to me.

Sonnet xi., " The Love Letter," is one of the most gracious of the series.   Its commencement—

> " Warmed by her hand and shadowed by her hair
>   As close she leaned and poured her heart through thee."

And the last of the following lines is exquisite—

> " Fain had I watched her when, at some fond thought,
>   Her bosom to the writing closelier prest ;
>   *And her breast's secrets peered into her breast.*"

The sonnet is, however, marred by a conceit worthy of the days of Donne, if not of Lyly or Marino, when the ink with which the letter is written is described as

> " The smooth black stream, that makes thy whiteness fair."

That adoration is apt to employ the language of half-fantastic hyperbole is granted.   The very exercise of coercing all existing things to yield homage to his mistress, or to join in the song in her praise, is a delightfulsome task. A comparison or illustration that satisfies the lover, but will not reach others, is better omitted from recorded praise, and such an illustration is here supplied.   Condemnation has been passed upon Rossetti for the use of language that is too ornate and elaborate.   Mr. Sharp, even, an acute and appreciative critic, censures the substitution for the simple words disease and misfortune of two such lines as—

> " What smouldering senses in death's sick delay
>   Or seizure of malign vicissitude."

The employment of language such as this is characteristic, and is more easily defensible than conceits such as
that instanced. If not defensible *per se* it is at least
paralleled in the work of the greatest poets. When for
Pharaoh and his host Milton substitutes—

> " Busiris and his Memphian chivalry"—

an instance in every way analogous, it is accepted as a
beauty. There is a place for rhetorical grace, and when
the association ennobles, its presence has a special appropriateness. It is under the influence of the most
overmastering passion that Othello likens, in some of the
nobliest lines ever penned, his bloody thoughts to—

> " The Pontic Sea
> Whose icy current and compulsive course
> Ne'er feels retiring ebb, but keeps due on
> To the Propontic and the Hellespont "—

words by some occult but true theory of fitness selected
for their grandeur of sound ; and it is in a similar spirit
that Macbeth uses the marvellous phrase—

> " No ; this my hand will rather
> The multitudinous seas incarnadine."

" Youth's Antiphony " (Sonnet xiii.) is delightful
prattle of lovers in sonnet form. That which follows,
" Youth's Spring Tribute," has an idea almost fit to put
beside Mr. Swinburne's unsurpassable lines—

> "The Spring begun
> Thy growth ere April had half done
> With the soft secret of her ways."

After spreading out the hair of his mistress on the bank, and watching through the golden tresses the wood-flowers bashful-eyed, the sonnet continues—

> "On these debatable borders of the year
> Spring's foot half falters; scarce she yet may know
> The leafless blackthorn-blossom from the snow."

It is impossible to go seriatim through sonnets almost all of which claim separate notice and commendation. A few only can be mentioned. "Love-Sweetness" stands conspicuous by its avowed preference for "the confident heart's still fervour," over the "sweet dimness of her loosened hairs downfall," her "mouths culled sweetness," and all the fragrant perfections of bodily presence on which the poet dwells. It is, indeed, advanced by Rossetti himself, as a complete answer to the charge of "fleshliness." Sonnet xxiv., "Pride of Youth," is the first that indicates the kind of regret indicated by Keats in the "Ode to the Nightingale"—

> "Where beauty cannot keep her lustrous eyes,
> Nor young love pine for them beyond to-morrow."

In the concluding sestett of this Rossetti draws attention to the change, familiar to every lover of Nature, that gives the hint of decay before the ripeness is obtained, that plants the first wrinkle on the brow of beauty before its maturity is reached, and the sere leaf on the same branch as the blossom.

> " There is a change in every hour's recall,
>   And the last cowslip in the fields we see
>   On the same day with the first corn-poppy.
>   Alas for hourly change !   Alas for all
>   The loves that from his hand, proud Youth lets fall,
>   Even as the beads of a told rosary "

In " Heart's Compass " (Sonnet xxvii.), he places himself once more in the most spiritual of moods, to see his mistress the meaning of all beauty, and in so seeing, to liken her to Love, whose name she is.

> " Sometimes thou seem'st not as thyself alone,
>   But as the meaning of all things that are ;
>   A breathless wonder, shadowing forth afar,
>   Some heavenly solstice, hushed and halcyon."

In " Her Gifts " (Sonnet xxxi.), he recounts once more the perfections of his mistress.   None of his poems is more eloquent in praise than this.   Once more the ennobling touch comes after the record of physical and intellectual attraction.

> " These are her gifts, as tongue may tell them o er,
>   Breathe low her name, my soul, for that means more."

Adoration can scarcely be expressed in language at once more vague if measured, yet more charged with expression and suggestion. "Secret Parting" (Sonnet xlv.), descriptive of the pained ecstasy of a meeting which is to be the last, contrasts finely in its tender melancholy with the burning and scornful outbreak in "Parted Love," which stands next in order. From this point regret and sorrow triumph over jubilancy. The sole joy in the four fine sonnets, with the sub-title of "Willow Wood," is that derived from dreams which bring a momentary and shadowy bliss, and leave the soul more desolate than before. While not less fine in execution, the sonnets included in the second part of the "House of Life," are less easily read, and on the whole less fervent than those by which they are preceded. Sometimes the thoughts, as in "Inclusiveness" (Sonnet lxiii.), are exquisitely painful, and show a tendency to dwell upon subjects almost morbidly distressing, as—

> "What man has bent o'er his son's sleep to brood
> How that face shall watch his when cold it lies?—
> Or thought as his own mother kissed his eyes,
> Of what her kiss was when his father wooed?"

In "Known in Vain" (Sonnet lxv.), a hopeless love finds despairing utterance, the termination being inexplicably sad.

> "Ah! who shall dare to search through what sad maze,
> Thenceforth their incommunicable ways,
> Follow the desultory feet of Death?"

The three sonnets, "The Choice," contrast with

the counsel, "watch and pray," the Biblical phrase
—"to-morrow thou shalt die." "Souls' Beauty"
(Sonnet lxxvii.), typifies under the guise of a personal
affection, the beauty that he has followed daily with
heart and feet "how passionately and irretrievably!"
One more instance, the last to be quoted, of the
deep sorrow which is breathed by the late sonnets,
is furnished in Sonnet lxxxiv., entitled "Farewell to
the Glen." The sestett portion of this is as follows—

> "And yet farewell ! Far better shalt thou fare
>   When children bathe sweet faces in thy flow ;
> And happy lovers blend sweet shadows there
>   In hours to come, than when an hour ago
> Thine echoes had but one man's sighs to bear,
>   And thy trees whispered what he feared to know."

Though intended to reflect, and in fact reflecting,
varying moods of Rossetti's mind, these sonnets convey
no idea of his ordinary mental attitude. Except in the
few closing years of his life, he was anything rather than
a melancholy man. He had with Jaques, "Neither the
scholar's melancholy, which is emulation ; nor the
musician's, which is fantastical ; nor the courtier's, which
is proud ; nor the soldier's, which is ambitious ; nor the
lawyer's, which is politic ; nor the lady's, which is nice ;
nor the lover's—which is all these." He had not, indeed,
like the famous philosopher of Arden, a melancholy of
his own, "compounded by many simples." His general
mood was joyous, if not absolutely mirthful, and the fits
of depression to which he was subject were wholly

attributable to the influence of narcotics. Few books took a stronger hold upon him than Mr. Gilbert's " Bab Ballads," the grotesque rhymes of which he was un wearied in quoting.

CHAPTER XV.

IN the Collected Edition of Rossetti's works, edited by
his brother, and published when the foregoing
remarks had been written, there appear a few works of
more interest than importance, which are not included
in the previous volumes. So exigent was Rossetti with
regard to his own work, and so careful in rejecting whatever did not reach the high standard of his own judgment,
his *reliquiæ* were sure to repay investigation. In future
times, no doubt, the ghouls, whose dismal and self-
imposed task it is to drag to light what the poet has
buried out of sight, will exercise their wicked will with
Rossetti. In the two volumes, however, of 1886, are
contained all for which the genuine lover of the great
poet will ask.

The addition of highest interest consists of " Henry
the Leper," the translation of the curious Swabian
poem of Hartmann Von Auë. Supremely tender and
touching, and curiously characteristic of the days of
mediæval thought, is this poem, in which, as in "Patient
Grizzle," and other works of a similar date, the lesson is
taught that the highest grace and privilege of womanhood
consist in submission to man, or sacrifice on his behalf.

The little maiden of humble birth in " Henry the Leper,"
hearing that the cure of her master, a nobleman, can only
be wrought by the sacrifice for him of life by a virgin,
offers herself up to die on his behalf.   In the true spirit
of mediæval legend the sacrifice is accompanied by a
species of exposure, from which maidenhood recoils with
as much fear as from death itself.   The physician of the
great school of Salerne, by whom the deed is to be
executed, points this out to her, and endeavours to dis-
suade her from the sacrifice.

> " Bethink thee—and consider thereof—
>   How the pains thou tempt'st are hard and rough.
>   First, with thy limbs naked and bare,
>   Before mine eyes thou must appear,—
>   So needs shall thy maiden shame be sore :
>   Yet still must thy woe be more and more,
>   What time thou art bound by heel and arm,
>   And with sharp hurt and with grievous harm
>   I cut from out thy breast the part,
>   That is most alive—even thine heart.
>   With thine eyes thou shalt surely see
>   The knife ere it enter into thee."

Noways dissuaded from the accomplishment of her
resolution, she urges upon the leech the necessity of
proceeding with the operation.   Reluctantly he consents,
and bids her take her raiment off.

> " Then was her heart joyous enough,
>   And she obeyed, and in little space
>   Stood up before the old man's face
>   As naked as God had fashioned her :
>   Only her innocence clothèd her :

> She fear'd not, and was not asham'd,
> In the sight of God standing unblamed ;
> To whom her dear life without price
> She offered up for a sacrifice."

More merciful than the ordinary writers of pious legend, or the compilers of the lives of saints, Hartmann von Auë spares the girl her martyrdom. Her lord, at the last moment, refuses to permit the accomplishment of the sacrifice, and, thanks to her humbling of his proud spirit, and the maiden's incessant and fervent prayers, the leprosy is removed without the purgation of the blood of the heroine. A full reward for her sufferings is provided when her master takes her for his wife. This notion—truly masculine—of recompense, lasted until the days of Richardson, whose Pamela is similarly rewarded for heroism of another sort, and still influences our literature.

The prose works first collected include the " Hand and Soul ;" the portion of Gilchrist's " Life of Blake" contributed by Rossetti ; the article contributed to *The Athenæum* in reply to Mr. Buchanan, entitled the " Stealthy School of Criticism ;" some criticisms on poems and pictures ; " The Orchard Pit "—the prose framework of a poem ; and " Saint Agnes of Intercession," an eminently interesting fragment, not, probably, without autobiographical significance. Many short poems and translations, gnomes, apothegms, &c., are also given. For most of these the world will be thankful. There is, however, nothing that furnishes any further insight into Rossetti's character, or reveals a new facet of his powers.

No such gratification as attended the publication of the first volume of poems was in store for him when the second appeared. The reception was not less cordial, and the enthusiasm of Rossetti's admirers was jarred by no discordant note. He was, however, incapable of being deeply stirred by any active emotion, at least of a selfish nature. A visit, in 1881, with his friend, Mr. Hall Caine, to the Vale of St. John, in Cumberland, failed to bring any permanent advantage to his health. Upon his return, indeed, he was even weaker than before.

One evening, after being cheered by the society of his dear friends, Dr. Westland Marston and his son, Mr. Philip Bourke Marston (whose recent and premature death is a loss to literature), Rossetti discovered that a portion of one side had become partially paralyzed. From this he made a partial recovery. It was none the less the beginning of the end. Early in 1872 he profited by the offer of a villa at Birchington-on-Sea which was made him by his friend, Mr. Seddon. Here he removed with Mr. Hall Caine; hither he was followed by his mother and his sister Christina; and here the end came. Into the particulars of his illness and death, which have been fully described by Mr. Hall Caine in his admirably sympathetic "Recollections of Dante Gabriel Rossetti," there is no need to enter. A moment's intrusion of self, which brings with it a clear insight into the graciousness and tenderness of Rossetti, is pardonable in the present writer, whose purpose has been not to intrude on the reader his own individuality. A review of Rossetti's new volume of poems, contributed by the present writer to the French magazine *Le Livre*, of which he was at that time the English correspondent, elicited from Rossetti a late, if not the last letter he wrote. This it is permissible to quote in full. It was accompanied by a reprint, dated 1881, of the volume of 1870, in which alterations, some of them named in the letter, had been made :—

"WEST CLIFF BUNGALOW,

"BIRCHINGTON-ON-SEA, KENT.

"5 *March*, /82.

"MY DEAR KNIGHT,—Curiously enough, I had not till to-day seen *Le Livre* for December, and read (though I had heard of it from Watts) your generous and unforgetful praise of one whom you could not speak of more warmly if we met as often as I could wish. Of the article's purport I hardly have a right to speak further, but can more pardonably dwell on its true literary aculty. I do not gather, of course, whether the French is your own, or rendered by another. In either case, the tone could not be more akin to the language.

"I have come here for a short time, being much out of health. Watts is with me to-day, and sends his truest remembrances from the sofa where he is reading your article. I have not seen the Marstons for some time, but must try to do so on my return to London, and I do hope you and I may yet again foregather.

"I have been penning a few verses to-day in lack of other occupation. I write with this to Ellis and White to send you a copy of the new edition of my old poems. In 'Sister Helen' (which, I remember, you always liked) there is an addition which (though it sounds alarming at first) has quite secured Watts's suffrage.   With love from what is left of me,

" Yours affectionately,

" D. G. ROSSETTI."

On the 9th of the following April—Easter Day, 1882 —he died at Birchington, where his body is interred. Loving ministrations attended him, it is pleasant to think, to the last.   His mother, sister, and brother, Mr. Watts, Mr. Shield, and Mr. Hall Caine were with him, and Mrs. William Rossetti arrived at a moment following his death. So died Dante Gabriel Rossetti, and with him passed away a man whom the leader of a school of painting, the most opposed to his own, pronounced "the most interesting individuality that followed art."   This Rossetti was, but he was also much more.   He was a poet, a creator, a leader of men.   Few who came beneath the spell of his influence were able or desirous to shake it off.   To be his friend was, in a sense, to be his disciple.   It was next to impossible to resist the enthusiasm with which his convictions were expressed, the contagion of his bright, animated presence, the influence of his singularly winning voice.   Enemies, in the full sense of the word, he did not know.   Putting on one side the aggressive vanity of the second half of the first line, Landor's epitaph upon himself might almost have been written by Rossetti—

" I strove with none, for none was worth the strife :
  Nature I loved, and, after Nature, art :
 I warmed both hands before the fire of life :
   It sinks ; and I am ready to depart."

To the general public he was almost unknown, and ridiculous rumours concerning him prevailed and still prevail. In literary circles even, outside his own immediate surroundings, an idea has been formed that Rossetti was a species of æsthete, effeminate in manner and *précieux* in style. Nothing could be further from the mark. He was essentially virile and robust, a little stubborn, and dogmatic in tone. A friend—himself a poet—writes of him in the language most nearly approaching condemnation that one admitted to his intimacy could employ :—" I liked him much, though I was often irritated by his prejudices, and his strong language against this or that person or subject. He was *borné*, too, somewhat in his interests, both on canvas and in verse, and would not care for certain forms of literature and life which he adm'tted were worth caring for. . . . However, his talk was always full of interest, and of rare knowledge, and he himself, his pictures, and his house, all together, had, I think, an immense influence for good on us all, and on English art and work, being not insular, yet not unEnglish ; and bringing into our world new and delightful subjects, and a personal character very striking, and unusual, and loveable."

An exhaustive biography of Rossetti is not yet to be expected, since few men are equal to the task of estimating fully his work in two different branches. That Mr. Watts will write a literary biography is the hope of all who loved Rossetti. Mr. F. G. Stephens, Rossetti's old and close friend, is understood to be engaged upon a biography, which will review his career as a painter, and will finally settle the relative dates of his pictorial works.

The value of this as a contribution to a knowledge of Rossetti can scarcely be over-estimated. Of importance almost equal will be the publication of Rossetti's correspondence with his family, which Mr. William Rossetti purposes, at no distant date, to give to the world. In this, as has before been said, Rossetti is seen at his best. Affectionate always, earnest and playful in turns, expansive and strongly influenced by prevailing moods and fancies, he stands before us in his true nature, without a notion of concealment. But for the privileges of access to this correspondence the foregoing poor attempt to present to others Rossetti as he was seen by one for a period in his intimacy, could never have been attempted.

THE END.

INDEX.

———◆———

BIBLIOGRAPHY,
AND CATALOGUE OF PICTURES.

BY

JOHN P. ANDERSON

(British Museum).

I. WORKS.

The Collected Works of Dante Gabriel Rossetti. Edited, with preface and notes, by William M. Rossetti. In two vols., 1886, 8vo.
> Contains various items, poetry and prose, never before printed.

II. SINGLE WORKS.

Sir Hugh the Heron : A Legendary Tale, in four parts. [In verse.] London, 1843, 4to.
> Printed by Rossetti's grandfather, G. Polidori, for private circulation only.

The Early Italian Poets from Ciullo d'Alcamo to Dante Alighieri (1100-1200-1300), in the original metres, together with Dante's Vita Nuova, translated by D. G. Rossetti. London, 1861, 8vo.

Dante and his Circle ; with the Italian Poets preceding him (1100-1200-1300). A Collection of lyrics, edited and translated in the original metres, by D. G. Rossetti. Revised and rearranged edition. London, 1874, 8vo.

Notes on the Vita Nuova and Minor Poems of Dante, together with the New Life, and many of the Poems. New York, 1866, 12mo.
> The translation used in this edition of *The Vita Nuova* is that by D. G. Rossetti in *The Early Italian Poets*, published in 1861.

Poems by D. G. R. London, 1870, 8vo.
> An edition was published at Boston the same year.

——Second Edition. London, 1870, 8vo.

Poems. New Edition. London,
1881, 8vo.
    This is to a great extent the
same book as the Poems, 1870; but
by no means identical with it—some
compositions from the vol. of 1870
being removed, and others substituted.

Poems by D. G. R. Boston [U.S.],
1882, 8vo.

Poems. (*Tauchnitz Edition*, with
Memoir by Hueffer). Leipzig,
— 12mo.

Ballads and Sonnets, by D. G. R.
London, 1881, 8vo.
    There is also a Tauchnitz Edition,
1882, with Memoir by Hueffer, and
a Boston Edition, 1882.

III. MISCELLANEOUS.

The Germ : Thoughts towards
Nature in Poetry, Literature,
and Art. Nos. 1, 2. London,
1850, 8vo.
            [Continued as :]
Art and Poetry ; being Thoughts
towards Nature. Conducted
principally by Artists. Nos. 3,
4. London, 1850, 8vo.
    This now rare magazine only
reached four numbers ; the title of
The Germ after the issue of parts 1
and 2 was altered to Art and
Poetry. Christina, Dante, and Wil-
liam Rossetti contributed largely,
the latter being the editor. Dante
was the author of twelve contribu-
tions, as follows : Pt. 1, *Songs of one
Household* (*My Sister's Sleep*), and
Hand and Soul ; pt. 2, *The Blessed
Damozel* ; pt. 3, *The Carillon*, *Sea
Limits*, here called *From the Cliffs* :
Noon ; pt. 4, *Pax Vobis* (afterwards
reprinted as *World's Worth* in the
Poems, re-issue of 1881); and six
Sonnets—*A Virgin and Child*, *by
Hans Memmeling* ; *A Marriage of
St. Katherine*, *by the same* ; *A Dance
of Nymphs*, *by Mantegna* ; *A
Venetian Pastoral*, *by Giorgione* ;
*Angelica rescued from the Sea-
Monster*, *by Ingres*, and another
sonnet on the same. There are two
copies of *The Germ* in the Library of

the British Museum, parts 3 and 4
of one of which contains MS. notes
by W. M. Rossetti.

The Blessëd Damozel.—[*The Oxford and Cambridge Magazine*,
1856, pp. 713-715.]
    Written by Rossetti in his nine-
teenth year, and published for the
first time in *The Germ*.

Hand and Soul.
    First published in *The Germ*, after-
wards in pamphlet form, of which
only a few copies were printed, not
published, and finally, with some
alterations, in *The Fortnightly Review*, vol. viii., N.S., 1870, pp. 692-702.

Sister Helen.
    First published in the Dusseldorf
Annual, about 1853, at the request
of the editress, Mrs. Howitt. It re-
appeared with improvements in the
volume of Poems, 1870, and again in
1881.

The Burden of Nineveh.
    *The Oxford and Cambridge Maga-
zine*, 1856, pp. 512-516, afterwards in
the Poems, 1870 and 1881.

The Staff and Scrip.
    *The Oxford and Cambridge Maga-
zine*, 1856, pp. 771-775 ; afterwards in
the Poems, 1870 and 1881.

Life of William Blake, "Pictor
Ignotus." With Selections from
his poems and other writings,
by the late Alexander Gilchrist,
etc. 2 vols. London, 1863,
8vo.
    Alex. Gilchrist having died before
this book was published, his widow,
Anne Gilchrist, prepared it for the
press. D. G. Rossetti did all the
editing, in vol. ii., of Blake's writings
in prose and verse. He also wrote
certain passages in vol. i. The
details are traceable in D. G. R.'s
Collected Works.

——Another Edition. 2 vols.
London, 1880, 8vo.
    D. G. R.'s work in vol. i. of this
edition is slightly modified and extended beyond the first edition.

Of Life, Love, and Death : Sixteen
Sonnets— *Willowwood* (4), *Sleep-
less Dreams, Lost on Both Sides*,

Run and Won, A Superscription, Winged Hours, The Landmark, Broken Music, Lost Days, Known in Vain, Inclusiveness, and *New-born Death* (2).
> *Fortnightly Review,* vol. v., N.S., 1869, pp. 266-273.

An account of Ebenezer Jones, the poet.
> *Notes and Queries,* vol. v., 4th Series, 1870, p 154.

Exhibition of Modern British Art at the Old Water Colour Gallery.
> Rossetti wrote a notice for the *Critic,* December 1, 1850, p. 576.

Exhibition of Pictures at Lichfield House.
> Rossetti wrote a notice of the Exhibition for the *Spectator,* Aug. 30, 1851, pp. 835-837.

Exhibition of Sketches and Drawings in Pall Mall East.
> Rossetti wrote the notice for the *Spectator,* Sept. 6, 1851, pp. 859, 860.

Il Losario : Poema Eroico Romanesco, di Ser Francesco Polidori.
> Reviewed by Rossetti in the *Critic,* April 1, 1853, p. 181.

Madeline, with other poems and parables. By Thomas Gordon Hake.
> Reviewed by Rossetti in *The Academy,* Feb. 1, 1871, pp. 105-107.

On the Site of a Mulberry-Tree ; planted by William Shakespeare, felled by the Rev. F. Gastrell.
> *The Academy,* Feb. 15, 1871, p. 128.

Maclise's Character Portraits.
> Reviewed by Rossetti in *The Academy,* April 15, 1871, pp. 217-218.

The Stealthy School of Criticism.
> Rossetti's reply in *The Athenæum,* Dec. 16, 1871, to Robert Buchanan's article entitled "The Fleshly School of Poetry."

The Cloud Confines.
> *The Fortnightly Review,* vol. xi., N.S., 1872, pp. 14, 15.

Parables and Tales. By Thomas Gordon Hake.
> Reviewed by Rossetti in *The Fortnightly Review,* vol. xiii., N.S., 1873, pp. 537-542.

Sunset Wings. (Seven verses.)
> *The Athenæum,* May 24, 1873, p. 660.

Translations of two poems from Tommaseo—*The Young Girl* and *A Farewell.*
> *The Athenæum,* June 13, 1874, p. 793.

Sonnets of Three Centuries. Edited by T. Hall Caine. London, 1882, 4to.
> Contains several sonnets by Rossetti, one of which, "Raleigh's Cell in the Tower," is printed for the first time.

IV.

ILLUSTRATIONS TO BOOKS.

The Music Master : a love story, and Two Series of Day and Night Songs. By William Allingham. London, 1855, 8vo.
> Contains one illustration by Rossetti, *The Maids of Elfen-Mere,* one of the *Day and Night Songs.*

Poems by Alfred Tennyson. London, 1857, 8vo.
> The illustrations by Dante Gabriel Rossetti are to *The Lady of Shalott,* p. 75 ; *Mariana in the South,* p. 82 ; *The Palace of Art,* pp. 113 and 119 ; *Sir Galahad,* p. 305.

Goblin Market, and other poems, by Christina Rossetti. With two designs by D. G. Rossetti. Cambridge, 1862, 8vo.

Goblin Market, The Prince's Progress, and other Poems. With four designs by D. G. Rossetti. New edition. London, 1875, 8vo.

The Prince's Progress, and other poems, by Christina G. Rossetti. With two designs by D. G. Rossetti. London, 1866, 8vo.

V. APPENDIX.

Biography and Criticism.

Buchanan, Robert.—The Fleshly School of Poetry and other phenomena of the day. London, 1872, 8vo.

A reprint of Buchanan's article, which appeared in the *Contemporary Review*, Oct. 1871, with the signature "Thomas Maitland." This reprint is greatly enlarged by the addition of chapters attacking Swinburne and Baudelaire. Rossetti wrote a reply to the article in *The Athenæum* for Dec. 16, 1871, styled *The Stealthy School of Criticism.*

Burlington Fine Arts Club.—Burlington Fine Arts Club, 1883. Pictures, drawings, designs, and studies by the late Dante Gabriel Rossetti. London, 1883, 4to.

Mr. H. Virtue Tebbs took the principal part in compiling this Catalogue.

Caine, T. H. Hall.—Recollections of D. G. Rossetti. London, 1882, 8vo.

——A Disquisition on Dante Gabriel Rossetti's painting in oil, entitled "Dante's Dream," delivered at the Walker Art Gallery, Nov. 3, 1881. Liverpool, n.d., 4to.

Catalogue.—Catalogue of the remaining works of D. G. R. . . . which will be sold, by Messrs. Christie, Manson, and Woods, May 12, 1883. [London, 1883] 8vo.

Chesneau, Ernest.—La Peinture Anglaise, par E. C. Paris [1882]. 8vo.

References to Rossetti's paintings.

——The English School of Painting. Translated by L. N. Etherington. (*Fine Art Library.*) London, 1885, 8vo.

Encyclopædias. — Encyclopædia Britannica. Ninth edition, Edinburgh, 1886, 4to.

Rossetti, by Theodore Watts, vol. xx., pp. 857-861.

Ferrazzi, Jacopo.--Manuale Dantesca. 4 vols. Bassano, 1865-71, 8vo.

Contains various details about Rossetti's writings and designs on Dante.

Forman, H. Buxton.—Our Living Poets. An Essay in Criticism. London, 1871, 8vo.

Dante Gabriel Rossetti, pp. 185-225. (Reprinted from *Tinsley's Magazine*).

Gamberale, Luigi.—Poeti Inglesi e Tedeschi moderni o contemporanei; versioni di L. G. Firenze, 1881, 16mo.

Hamilton, Walter.—The Æsthetic Movement in England. London, 1882, 8vo.

Dante Gabriel Rossetti, pp. 54-60; Buchanan's Attack on Rossetti, pp. 60-64. [A second edition embodies some corrections, etc., communicated by W. M. Rossetti.]

Hueffer, Francis. — Italian and other Studies. London, 1883, 8vo.

Exhibitions of Rossetti's Pictures, pp. 83-105. Reprinted from the *Times*, Dec. 30, 1882, Jan. 13 and 15, 1883.

Ingram, John H.—Oliver Madox Brown. A biographical sketch, etc. London, 1883, 8vo.

Contains some matter relating to Rossetti, with a few letters to Oliver Madox Brown.

Myers, F. W. H.—Essays, Modern. London, 1883, 8vo.

Rossetti and the Religion of Beauty, pp. 312-334. [Reprinted from the *Cornhill Magazine*, 1883].

Nicholson Peter Walker.—The Round Table Series. No. vi., Dante Gabriel Rossetti, poet and painter. Edinburgh, 1886. 8vo.

Only one hundred copies of this edition printed.

Placci, Carlo. — Dante Gabriele Rossetti. (Reprinted from the *Rassegna Nazionale.*) Firenze, 1882. 8vo.

Rossetti, W. M.—Notes on the Royal Academy Exhibition, 1868. Part i., by W. M. R., Part ii., by A. C. Swinburne. London [1868], 8vo.
Swinburne on Rossetti's pictures, pp. 45-51.

Royal Academy.—Exhibition of Works, by the Old Masters, including a special selection from the works of John Linnell and Dante Gabriel Rossetti. Winter Exhibition, 1883. London [1883], 8vo.

Sarrazin, Gabriel. — Poètes Modernes de l'Angleterre. Paris, 1885, 8vo.
Dante Gabriel Rossetti, pp. 233-271.

Sharp, William.—Dante Gabriel Rossetti: a record and a study. London, 1882, 18mo.

Stedman, Edmund Clarence. — Victorian Poets. Boston, [U.S.], 1876, 8vo.
Latter-day Singers—Robert Buchanan, Dante Gabriel Rossetti, William Morris, pp. 342-378.

Swinburne, Algernon C.—Essays and Studies. London, 1875, 8vo.
The poems of Dante Gabriel Rossetti, pp. 60-109. [Reprinted from *The Fortnightly Review*, 1870.]

Tablettes.—Tablettes Biographiques. (Eighth Year.) Paris, 1882-3, 8vo.
Rossetti, by Ch. de Guillaumet.

Tirebuck, William. — Dante Gabriel Rossetti; His Work and Influence, including a brief survey of recent art tendencies. London, 1882, 8vo.

Ward, Thomas H.—The English Poets, etc. London, 1883, 8vo.
Dante Gabriel Rossetti, by Walter H. Pater, vol. iv., pp. 633-664.

POEMS SET TO MUSIC.

A Little While.—Poetry by D. G. Rossetti. Music by Florence A. Marshall. London [1870], fol.

A New Year's Burden. Song [begins "Along the grass"]. Words by D. G. R. Music by Lord Henry Somerset. London [1876], fol.

A New Year's Burden. Song [begins "Along the grass"]. Written by D. G. R. Music by Florence A. Marshall. London, [1877], fol.

A New Year's Burden. Duet [begins "Along the grass"]. Words by D. G. R. Music by Eaton Faning. London [1879], fol.

Love-Lily and other Songs, by D. G. R.—Love-Lily, Plighted Promise, A Young Fir-Wood, My Father's Close, Autumn Song, A Little While. Set to Music by Edward Dannreuther. London [1884], 8vo.

MAGAZINE ARTICLES.

Rossetti, Dante Gabriel.—Old and New, vol. 2, 1870, pp. 92-94. —Tinsley's Magazine, vol. 8, 1871, pp. 150-160.—Scribner's Monthly, by Edward C. Stedman, vol. 9, 1875, pp. 431-434. —Academy, by Edward Dowden, vol. 20, pp. 285, 286.—St. James's Magazine, by Thomas Bayne, vol. 32, 1877, pp. 415-430.—Unsere Zeit, by Mary F.

Rossetti, Dante Gabriel.
    Robinson, vol. 1, N.S., 1879,
pp. 767-778. — Century, with
portrait, by Edmund W. Gosse,
vol. 24, 1882, pp. 718-725.—
Harper's New Monthly Magazine, by Mary F. Robinson, vol.
65, 1882, pp. 691 - 701.—
Academy, by T. Hall Caine, vol.
21, 1882, pp. 266-268.— Art
Journal, by William Tirebuck,
1883, pp. 27, 28.—Quarterly
Review, vol. 132, 1872, pp. 59-
84 ; same article, Eclectic
Magazine, N.S., vol. 15, 1872,
pp. 385-399.
    —and Fleshly School of Poetry.
Contemporary Review, by
Thomas Maitland (Robert
Buchanan), vol, 18, 1871,
pp. 334-350.
    —"Fleshly School" Scandal.
Tinsley's Magazine, vol. 10,
1872, pp. 89-102.
    —and Tadema, Linnell, and
Lawson. Blackwood's Edin-
burgh Magazine, by J. B.
Atkinson, vol. 133, 1883, pp.
392-411.
    —and the Religion of Beauty.
Cornhill Magazine, by F. W. H.
Myers, vol. 47, 1883, pp. 213-
224 ; reprinted in Essays, etc.,
by Myers, 1883.
    —Art of. Contemporary Re-
view, by Harry Quilter, vol. 43,
1883, pp. 190-203.
    —Earlier Works of. Portfolio,
by F. G. Stephens, 1883, pp.
87-94 and 114-119.
    —English Pre - Raphaelite and
Poetical School of Painters. An-
dover Review, by Helen B. Mer-
riman, vol. 1, 1884, pp. 594-612.
    —Exhibitions of his Pictures.
Art Journal, 1883, pp. 61, 62.—
Pall Mall Gazette, Jan. 3, 1883.

Rossetti, Dante Gabriel.
    —Times, Jan. 13, 1883.—Athe-
næum, Jan. 6, 1883, pp. 22,
23.—Academy, by C. Monk-
house, vol. 23, 1883, pp. 14,
15, and 50, 51.
    —Influence in Art. English
Illustrated Magazine, by J.
Comyns Carr, 1883, pp. 28-40.
    —Memorials of. Atlantic
Monthly, vol. 51, 1883, pp. 549-
555.
    —Notes on his Works. Art
Journal, by W. M. Rossetti,
1884, pp. 148-152, 165-168,
204-208, 255.
    —Obituary Notices of. Athe-
næum, by Theodore Watts and
Fred. George Stephens, April
15, 1882, pp. 480-481.
    —On Some Marginalia made by
him in a copy of Keats's Poems.
Manchester Quarterly, by Geo.
Milner, vol. 2, 1883, pp. 1-10.
    —Painter and Poet. Putnam's
Monthly Magazine, by W. J.
Stillman, N.S. vol. 6, 1870,
pp. 95-101.
    —Parodied. Pall Mall Gazette,
Nov. 5, 1881.
    —Picture, "A Vision of Fiam-
metta." Athenæum, Oct. 5,
1878, pp. 439, 440.
    —Pictures of. Athenæum, Aug.
14, 1875, pp. 219-221 ; April
14, 1877, pp. 486, 487 ; Nov. 1,
1879, pp. 566, 567 ; Feb. 26,
1881, p. 304 ; Aug. 20, 1881,
p. 250.
    —Poems. Fortnightly Review,
by A. C. Swinburne, N.S., vol.
7, 1870, pp. 551-579.—Athenæum, April 1870, pp. 573, 574.
—Westminster Review, vol. 38,
N.S., 1870, pp. 226, 227 ; vol.
39, N.S., pp. 55-92. — North
American Review, by J. R. Den-

Rossetti, Dante Gabriel.

nett, vol. 111, 1870, pp. 471-480.
—Fraser's Magazine, by John
Skelton, vol. 1, N.S., 1870, pp.
609-622 ; same article, Littell's
Living Age, vol. 105, 1870, pp.
686-697 ; Eclectic Magazine, vol.
12, N.S., pp. 143-154.—New
Monthly Magazine, vol. 146,
1870, pp. 681-700.—Atlantic
Monthly, vol. 26, 1870, pp.
115-118. — Lakeside Monthly,
vol. 4, 1870, pp. 320-323.—
Nation, vol. 11, 1870, pp. 29, 30.
—North British Review, vol. 52,
1870, pp. 598-601.—Broadway,
vol. 1, 3rd series, 1870, pp. 286-
288.—St. James's Magazine,
by Frederick Wedmore, vol.
9, N.S., 1872, pp. 31-40. —
New Eclectic, vol. 7, p. 110.
—Catholic World, by J. C.
Earle, vol. 19, 1874, pp. 263-272.
—New Monthly Magazine, by
T. H. Hall Caine, vol. 116, 1879,
pp. 800-812.—Le Livre, by Jos.
Knight, 1881, pp. 722, 723.—
Critic, vol. 1, 1881, pp. 305,
306.—Pall Mall Gazette, Nov. 4,
1881.—Athenæum, Oct. 1881,
pp. 457-460 ; same article,
Eclectic Magazine, vol. 34,
N.S., 1881, pp. 851-858.—
Art Journal, by Alice
Meynell, 1882, pp. 85-87.—
Fraser's Magazine, by Thomas
Bayne, vol. 25, N.S., 1882, pp.
376-384 — Edinburgh Review,
vol. 155, 1882, pp. 322-337.
—British Quarterly Review,
vol. 76, 1882, pp. 109-127.—
Contemporary Review, by
Principal Shairp, vol. 42, 1882,
pp. 17-32.
——*The Painted Poetry of, and*

Rossetti, Dante Gabriel.

Watts. Nineteenth Century,
by Mrs. Barrington, vol. 13,
1883, pp. 950-970.
——*Pictorialism in Verse.* Port-
folio, by William Sharp, 1882,
pp. 176-180.
——*Pre-Raphaelite Brotherhood.*
Contemporary Review, by Wm.
Holman Hunt, vol. 49, 1886,
pp. 471-488, 737-750, and
820-833.
—— *Pre-Raphaelite Exhibition.*
Saturday Review, vol. 4, 1857,
pp. 11, 12.
—— *Pre-Raphaelite Magazine.*
Fraser's Magazine, by J.
Ashcroft Noble, vol. 25, N.S.,
1882, pp. 568-580.
——*Pre - Raphaelitism.* Nation,
vol. 1, 1865, pp. 273, 274.
——*Pre-Raphaelitism in Art and
Literature.* British Quarterly
Review, vol. 16, 1852, pp.
197-220.
——*Reaction from Pre-Raphael-
itism.* Fine Arts Quarterly
Review, by P. G. Hamerton,
vol. 2, 1864, pp. 255-262.
—— *Recollections of (Caine's).*
Nation, vol. 36, 1883, pp. 67-68.
——*A Record and a Study*
(*Sharp's*). Nation, vol. 36,
1883, p. 408.
——*Translations.* Nation, vol.
18, 1874, pp. 159, 160.—Na-
tional Review, vol. 15, 1862, pp.
60-95.—Fraser's Magazine, vol.
65, 1862, pp. 580-594.
—— *Truth about.* Nineteenth
Century, by Theodore Watts,
vol. 13, 1883, pp. 404-423.
——*Two Drawings by.* Nation,
vol. 3, 1866, pp. 501-502.

VI.—CHRONOLOGICAL LIST OF WORKS

VII.—CHRONOLOGICAL LIST OF PAINTING AND DRAWINGS.

1846.

1 *Pencil.*—Portrait of Wm. M. Rossetti.

1847.

2 *Pencil and White Chalk.*— Portrait study of the artist himself.

1848.

3 *Pen and Ink.*—"The sun may shine and we be cold."
4 ,, Gretchen in the Chapel.
5 ,, Genevieve.
6 ,, Sketch of himself.
7 *Sepia.*—"La Belle Dame sans mercy."
8 *Oil.*—Portrait of Professor Gabriele Rossetti (Father of the Artist).
9 ,, Portrait of Mrs. Banks.

1849.

10 *Oil.*—Girlhood of Mary Virgin.
11 *Pen and Ink.*—"The First Anniversary of the Death of Beatrice."
12 *Water Colour.*—The Laboratory from Browning. [Rossetti's First Water Colour.]
13 *Pen and Ink.* — "Il Saluto di Beatrice" (1849-50).

1850.

14 *Oil.*—Ecce Ancilla Domini.
15 *Water Colour.*—Small upright figure in red [Rosso-vestita].
16 *Pen and Ink.*—"Taurello's First Sight of Fortune" (from Browning's "Sordello"), 1850-51.

17 *Crayons.*—Study of Two Girls Dancing.
18 *Pencil.*—Designs for No. 19.
19 *Water Colour.* — Morning Music.
20 *Pen and Ink.*—Dorothy and Theophilus
21 ,, Several portraits, etc.

1851.

22 *Water Colour.* — Beatrice, meeting Dante at a marriage feast, denies him her salutation.
23 *Indian Ink.*—Bethlehem Gate [c. 1851].
24 *Water Colour.*—The Queen's Page.
25 *Pencil and Black Chalk.*—A little Girl dancing [c. 1851].
26 *Pencil.*—How they met themselves. See Nos. 108, 174. [Original sketch destroyed or lost.]
27 *Pen and Ink.* — Hesterna Rosa, No. 1.
28 ,, Boy and Girl dancing.
29 *Water Colour.* — Lucrezia Borgia playing on a lute, with dancing children, etc.

1852.

30 *Water Colour.* — "Fazio's Mistress." See Nos. 166, 173.
31 ,, Giotto painting the portrait of Dante.
32 ,, The Annunciation [unfinished].
33 ,, The Meeting of Dante and Beatrice in the Purgatorio.
34 *Oil.*—The Two Mothers.

35 *Pencil.*—Head of Ford Madox Brown.
36 *Crayon.*—William Bell Scott —head.

1853.

37 *Pen and Ink.* — "Found.' [Early study for the oil picture begun this year, and unfinished in 1882.]
38 ,, Another sketch, supposed to be earlier.
39 ,, Sketch of the artist's Mother.
40 ,, Two Designs in one frame [c. 1853]. "Fra Angelico Painting." Giorgione painting from a model.
41 ,, A little Girl wheeling Baby in a Trundle.
42 *Pencil.*—Sketch of the Artist's Father.
43 ,, Girl reclining on a pillow.
44 *Water Colour.*—Dante at the Anniversary of Beatrice's Death.
45 ,, Carlisle Tower.
46 ,, Female Figure singing to a Lute.
47 *Ink.*—Portrait of himself.

1854.

48 *Pen and Ink and Pencil.*— Miss E. Siddal.
49 *Pencil.*— do.
50 ,, Paolo and Francesca. [Study for the first compartment of Triptych, No. 142.]
51 *Water Colour.* — Paolo and Francesca.
52 ,, Arthur's Tomb; or, the Last Meeting of Lancelot and Guenevere.
53 *Pencil.*—The Maids of Elfen-Mere. [See No. 61.]

1855.

54 *Water Colour.*—Chapel before the Lists.

55 *Pen and Ink.* — Hamlet and Ophelia.

56 *Water Colour.* — Portrait of Miss Siddal.

57 „ "La Belle Dame sans mercy."

58 „ Dante's Dream at the time of the death of Beatrice.

59 *Pen and Ink.* — Sketch of Alfred Tennyson reading " Maud."

60 „ Another sketch of do.

61 *On Wood.*—Illustration to Allingham's Poems. [Same as No. 53.]

62 *Water Colour.*—The Passover —the Holy Family. [? 1855, unfinished.]

63 *Pen and Ink.*—Cats' Cradle. [*c.* 1855.]

1856-57.

64 *Pencil.* — Bride and Bridegroom [*c.* 1856.]

65 *Oil.* — King René's Honeymoon [Panel in a Cabinet].

66 „ St. Catherine.

67 *Pen and Ink.* — Morte d' Arthur.

68 *Water Colour.*—The Tune of Seven Towers. [See Defence of Guenevere. W. Morris, p. 199.]

69 „ The Gate of Memory. [Retouched 1864.]

70 „ Wedding of St. George.

71 „ Fra Pace.

72 *On Wood.*—Five Tennyson Engravings. [Existing also as water colours, but Mr. W. M. Rossetti doubts whether the St.

Cecilia or the Arthur and Queens exist as water colours.]

73 *Water Colour.* — The Blue Closet.

74 „ The Bower Garden.

75 *Fresco.* — Lancelot at the Shrine of the Sanct Grael.

76 *Black Chalk.*—A Fawn [*c.* 1857].

77 *Water Colour.*—Sir Galahad. [No. 1.]

78 *Water Colour.*—Sanct Grael.

79 „ Death of Breuse sans Pitié.

80 „ St. Cecilia [see No. 72].

81 „ *Chalk Design.*—St. Luke. The Painter.

82 *Water Colour.*—Meeting of Sir Tristram and Yseult.

83 *Pencil.*—Mary in the House of John.

84 „ Head of a Scotch Girl. [*c.* 1856.]

85 *Pen and Ink.*—Mary Magdalene at the door of Simon the Pharisee.

1858.

86 *Indian Ink.*—Queen Guenevere. [A study for the figure of Guenevere in the Union Building, Oxford.]

87 *Water Colour.*—A Christmas Carol. [See Nos. 219 and 220.]

88 „ Mary in the House of John. [See No. 105.]

89 „ Ruth and Boaz.

90 „ Golden Water.

91 *Ink.*—Mary Magdalene, etc.

92 *Water Colour.* — Passover Drawing.

93 *Pen and Ink.*—Sketch of Miss Siddal.

94 *Pencil.*—Finished Study of a Girl's Head (Ada). [*c.* 1858.]
95 „ Outline Study of a Girl's Head (Ada). [*c.* 1858].
96 „ Sketch of a Girl asleep on a Sofa [*c.* 1858].
97 „ Study of a boy, Christ.

1859.

98 *Water Colour.* — My Lady Greensleeves.
99 *Water Colour and Oil.*— Head of Christ.
100 „ Mary Magdalene at the Door. [Replica.]
101 *Crayons.* — Beata Beatrix. [First study for No. 163.]
102 *Oil.*—Dante and Beatrice.
103 *Pencil.*—Study for the following
104 *Oil.*—Bocca Baciata.
105 *Water Colour.*—Mary in the House of John. [Replica of No. 87.]
106 „ Portrait of Robert Browning.
107 „ Triptych for Llandaff Cathedral. [Coloured study for No. 132.]

1860.

108 *Ink.*—How they met themselves. [Finished design. See Nos. 26 and 174.]
109 *Pencil.*—Portrait of Mrs. Ford Madox Brown.
110 *Pen and Ink.*—Dr. Johnson and the Methodist Ladies at the Mitre.
111 *Water Colour.*—do.
112 *Pencil.* — Mr. Swinburne (head and shoulders.)-
113 *Oil.*—Portrait of Mr. Swinburne.

114 *Indian Ink.*—Dantis Amor. [*c.* 1860. This design was carried out as a panel painting.]
115 *Pencil.* — Signor Giuseppe Maenza (head).
116 „ Portrait of Mrs. D. G. Rossetti.
117 „ Aspecta Medusa.
118 *Indian Ink.*—A Fight for a Woman. [Design for No. 196.]

1861.

119 *Oil.*—Portrait of Mrs. D. G. Rossetti.
120 *Water Colour.*—Portrait of do.
121 *Pencil.* — Portrait of do. standing at an easel.
122 „ Miss E. Burne Jones.
123 *Water Colour.* — Leah and Rachel.
124 *Oil.*—Burd-Alane.
125 *Pen and Ink.*— Cassandra. Retouched, 1869.
126 *Oil.*—Portrait of Mrs. J. A. Heaton.
127 *Red Chalk.*—Portrait of John Ruskin.
128 *Oil.*—Fair Rosamond.
129 *Water Colour.* — Farmer's Daughter.
130 *Crayons.*—Regina Cordium.
131 „ Penelope.
132 *Oil.*—The Triptych for Llandaff Cathedral. [See No. 107.]
133 *Pencil.*—Mrs. H. T. Wolf, after Death.
134 „ Lachesis. [Study of a lady seated, holding a thread.]
135 *Water Colour.* — Lucrezia Borgia.
136 „ Sir Galahad. [Replica of No. 77.]

316 *Oil.*—Proserpina. [See Nos.
    353, 386, 393.]
317 *Water Colour.*—Rosa Triplex.
    [Replica of No. 269.]
318 *Crayons.*—Portrait of Mr. W.
    Theodore Watts.
319 *Oil.*—The Damozel of the
    Sanct Grail.
320 *Crayons.*—¾-length Study.
321 ,, Portrait Study, in profile.
    (Lady.)
322 ,, Two Female Heads.
323 *Black Chalk.*—Dante (full
    length). [Study for No.
    366.]
324 *Oil.*—Portrait of Mrs. Morris.
325 *Crayons.*—Portrait of Mrs.
    William Rossetti.
326 *Pencil.*—Life-size Head Study
    (Lady).

1875.
327 *Crayons.*—Washing Hands
    [different to No. 199 ;
    study for No. 328].
328 *Oil.*—La Bella Mano.
329 *Crayons.*—The Blessèd Damo-
    zel. [Study for No. 351.]
330 *Pencil.*—The Question. [Or
    the Sphinx.]
331 *Oil.*—Pandora. [See No. 261.]
332 *Crayons.*—A Winged Cherub.
333 *Pencil.*—Portrait of a Lady.
334 *Crayons.*—Astarte Syriaca.
335 *Pen and Ink.*—   do.
    [Study for No. 349.]
336 *Crayons.*—Study of an Angelic
    Head.
337 ,.   do.
338 ,, Portrait of Mrs. C. A.
    Howell.
339 ,, Female Figure. [Study
    for *Dante's Dream,* No.
    366.]
340 ,, Study for central portion
    of do.
341 ,, Portrait of Mrs. Stillman.

342 *Crayons.*—Dante's Awakening
    from his Dream. [Study
    for one of the predella
    subjects to No. 366.]
343 ,, The Sea-Spell. [Study for
    No. 350.]
344 ,, Figure and Twilight Land-
    scape. [Study for predella
    to the Blessèd Damozel.]
345 *Pencil.*—A Vision of Fiam-
    metta. [Study for No.
    367.]
346 *Crayons.*—Three Studies for
    Heads of do.
347 ,, Head Studies for Astarte.
348 ,, Mrs. Gabriele Rossetti.
    [Head and Bust.]

1876-7.
349 *Oil.*—Astarte Syriaca.
350 ,, The Sea-Spell.
351 ,, The Blessèd Damozel.
    No. 1. [See No. 377.]
352 *Crayons.*—Domizia Scaligera.
    [*c.* 1876.]
353 *Oil.*—Proserpina. [Replica.
    See No. 316.]
354 *Crayons.* — A Magdalene.
    (Head.)
355 ,, The Spirit of the Rainbow.
356 ,, Forced Music.
357 ,, The Salutation (Head
    Study of No. 392.]
358 ,, Mnemosyne. [Finished
    Study of No. 385.]
359 *Oil.*—Mary Magdalene.
360 *Crayons.*—Gretchen. Study
    of a head. [See No. 390.]

1878.
361 *Crayons.*—Pandora [Replica].
362 ,, Study of a Female Head.
363 ,, Perlascura.
364 ,, Portrait of Christina Ros-
    setti.
365 ,, Mrs. Rossetti, sen., and
    Miss Rossetti.

The dates of some of these works must be regarded as conjectural only. There are cases in which absolute certainty is impossible.

PHOTOGRAPHS WHICH HAVE BEEN PUBLISHED AFTER WORKS BY ROSSETTI.

From Oil Pictures.

1. The Girlhood of Mary Virgin.
2. The Beloved.
3. Lilith.
4. Dante's Dream (the larger oil-picture).
5. Mrs. William Morris.
6. Gabriele Rossetti (Portrait of D. G. Rossetti's Father, 1848).
7. Proserpina.
8. Mnemosyne.

From Water-Colours.

9. Dante drawing an Angel in memory of Beatrice.
10. Rosa Triplex.
11. Washing Hands.
12. Borgia (seated lady with dancing children).

From Designs.

13. Beatrice dead—Crayon.
14. Head of Dante— do.
15. Head of one of the attendant Ladies--Crayon.

(From Dante's Dream.)

16. The Sphinx—Pencil.
17. Hesterna Rosa—Pen and ink.
18. Cassandra—Pen and ink.
19. La Donna della Fiamma—Crayon.
20. How they met themselves—Pen and ink.
21. Pandora—Crayon for the oil-picture.
22. Hamlet and Ophelia—Pen and ink.
23. The Sonnet—Rossetti's sonnet on The Sonnet, with illustrative design—Pen and ink.
24. The Prince's Progress—Two designs for Christina Rossetti's poem—Pen and ink.
25. Mary Magdalene at the door of Simon the Pharisee—Pen and ink.
26. The Parable of the Vineyard—Seven separate designs—Cartoons for stained glass.
27. La Donna della Finestra—Crayon.
28. The death of Lady Macbeth—Pencil.
29. Same subject—Pen and ink.
30. Design from an Old Ballad—Indian ink.
31. Three designs from Tennyson's Poems, for the Woodcuts—Indian ink.
32. The Sancgreal — Design intended for the Union Building, Oxford—Pen and ink.
33. The Salutation of Beatrice—Crayon.
34. Lovers Kissing—Pencil.
35. Troy Town—Indian ink.
36. Design for Title of Early Italian Poets—Pen and ink.
37. Dantis Amor—Indian ink.
38. "Found"—Study of the man's head—Pencil.
39. Sister Helen—Pen and ink.
40. Desdemona's Death - Song—Pen and ink.
41. From the Blessèd Damozel. (Lovers embracing)—Pencil.
42. do. —(A different group)—Pencil.
43. Orpheus and Eurydice--Pencil.

44. The Sea-Spell—First Sketch for the Picture—Pen and ink.

PORTRAITS AND HEADS.

45. Mrs. Rossetti (Senior) and Miss Christina Rossetti—Crayon.
46. Mrs. Rossetti (Senior)—Pen and ink.
47. Miss Christina Rossetti (half-length)—Crayon.
48. The same (head)—Crayon.
49. Miss Herbert—Pencil.
50. William Bell Scott—Crayon.
51. Algernon Charles Swinburne —Pencil.

Mrs. Dante Rossetti Series.

52. Full Figure ; two separate drawings—Pencil.

53. Standing Figure—Pen and ink.
54. Half-figure at easel—Pencil.
55. Head—Pen and ink.
56. Head—Pencil.

Perlascura Series.

57. Lachesis—Pencil.
58. Queen Guenevere—Indian ink.
59. The Roseleaf—Pencil.
60. The Couch—Pen and ink.
61. Head ; three separate drawings—Crayon.

The Scotch Girl Series.

62. The Laurel—Pencil.
63. Profile—Pencil.
64. The Hair-net—Pencil.